BLACKWELL'S GERMAN TEXTS

General Editor: ALEXANDER GILLIES

EDUARD MÖRIKE

POEMS

Selected and Edited by

LIONEL THOMAS, M.A., PH.D.

BASIL BLACKWELL · OXFORD

1979

ISBN 0 631 01660 0

Fourth impression, 1980

Printed and bound in Great Britain at
The Camelot Press Ltd, Southampton

1432478   MORIKE,E.   Poems.

831 MOR PR.   6.84   £4.25

Please renew/return this item by the last date shown.

So that your telephone call is charged at local rate,
please call the numbers as set out below:

	From Area codes 01923 or 0208:	From the rest of Herts:
Renewals:	01923 471373	01438 737373
Enquiries:	01923 471333	01438 737333
Minicom:	01923 471599	01438 737599

831
MOR
MOR

L32b

So that your telephone call is charged at local rate,
please call the numbers as set out below:

L33

CONTENTS

INDEX OF FIRST LINES

vii

PREFACE

In presenting this selection of Mörike's poems the editor has tried to meet what he believes to be a real need for an English edition with notes on interpretation and linguistic difficulties. In recent years Mörike's poetry has been the subject of much painstaking and scholarly analysis in Germany, and many of the books and articles which have appeared in the post-war period have contributed greatly to a deeper understanding of his work. Mörike is not an easy poet, particularly for foreign readers, and his poems demand the closest study to be even partially appreciated. The editor hopes that his notes, based on published material, will at least provide a starting-point from which the student in British schools or universities can work towards a deeper perception of the poet's qualities. Considerations of space have not made it possible to include all the poems which have their champions among Mörike enthusiasts, but an attempt has been made to compile a selection representative of the great variety of theme and treatment to be found in his poetry.

Although in the past most editors of selections or editions of Mörike's poems have adhered to the arrangement accepted by the poet, the editor has decided to adopt a chronological arrangement in accordance with the year in which the first version was composed. To do so is no impiety, for Mörike showed little interest in the ordering of his poems for publication, accepting the sequence suggested by Hermann Kurz; his grouping, which underlines parallels and contrasts among the poems, gave a confused impression which, as Karl Fischer remarks, irritates both general reader and researcher. A chronological ordering has the advantage for the student that it enables him (or her) to follow Mörike's progress as a poet and throws into prominence the periods of outstanding productivity; it also reveals the difference in his works at various times, e.g. up to 1834, in the years 1834–43, and in the creative phase of middle age. Since the exact dates of composition for several poems are controversial, tentative dates have been given in some cases. Only in the case of 'An meinen Vetter' has the usual arrangement been deliberately ignored, so that the two inseparable poems can be studied together. References are given to Baumann's edition because, unlike that of Mayne, it is still easily obtainable. When *Maler Nolten* is mentioned, the reference is to the 1832 edition unless otherwise stated.

The editor's thanks are due to Professor Boyd for his assistance in facilitating the publication of this work; to Professor Gillies for reading the manuscript, and suggesting improvements; to his wife for her interest and encouragement; and to Dr. Lösel for practical help in reading the proofs and for making several valuable suggestions.

L. H. C. THOMAS.

DUBLIN

September 1958

INTRODUCTION

(For details of works mentioned, see Bibliography. Reference is made occasionally, both in the Introduction and in the Notes, to poems not included in the selection.)

EDUARD MÖRIKE, fourth child of the doctor Karl Friedrich Mörike and his wife Charlotte, was born in Ludwigsburg on September 8, 1804. Here he spent his childhood and early youth, attending the *Lateinschule* at the same time as his future friends Friedrich Theodor Vischer and David Friedrich Strauß. When his father died in 1817, the family moved to Stuttgart, where his education and upbringing were watched over by his uncle Eberhard Friedrich Georgii, a distinguished and cultured man who had many learned friends and a fine library. Eduard now attended the *Gymnasium illustre*, where, encouraged by his uncle, he began to lay the foundations of that rich knowledge and profound grasp of Greek and Latin literatures which were to be an important source of inspiration to him as a poet. Translating from ancient languages into verse-forms, the usual practice of the time, may well have stimulated his interest in versification.

In 1818 Eduard gained a place in the *Klosterschule* at Urach, one of the famous Protestant seminaries which were the best schools in Württemberg; these produced men of great distinction, especially in the fields of literature, philosophy and theology.[1] At Urach he met as fellow pupils Wilhelm Waiblinger, Wilhelm Hartlaub and Johannes Mährlen; Waiblinger was to be a close associate at the university, Hartlaub and Mährlen devoted and sympathetic friends of a lifetime. In 1822 he entered the theological college (*Stift*) at Tübingen; here he found a congenial companion in Ludwig Bauer, with whom he sought to escape the boredom of academic routine in creating the mythical land of Orplid. It was in 1823 that he fell in love with the mysterious Maria Meyer, who had been a member of the wandering sect of Julia von Krüdener until the Swiss government put an end to her activities; since Maria had left home against the wishes of her parents, they insisted that

[1] E.g. Hegel, Schelling, Hölderlin, Wilhelm Hauff, D. F. Strauß, F. Th. Vischer, Hermann Kurz.

xi

she should, as a kind of penance, take work as a servant. Mörike first met her when she was working temporarily as a barmaid in Ludwigsburg; both he and his student friend Rudolf Lohbauer were fascinated by her enigmatic personality, and although Lohbauer is said to have declared many years later, 'Mörike und ich haben uns damals in eine ganz inferiore Person vergafft',[1] Mörike's passion for Maria and his struggles to overcome what must have been regarded by his friends and relatives as a senseless infatuation were shattering personal experiences from which he distilled the strangely beautiful and passionate cycle of poems, 'Peregrina'.

Mörike suffered great loss through the death of his brother August in 1824 (see 'An eine Äolsharfe'), and of his favourite sister Luise in 1827. Having completed his studies in 1826, he was appointed curate at Oberboihingen. Up to this point Mörike and his advisers had thought less of the vocational aspect of a career in the Church than of the sound education provided inexpensively by *Klosterschule* and *Stift*. Now there began for Mörike a period of wandering from one meanly paid and subordinate post to another (Möhringen, Köngen, Pflummern, Plattenhardt, Owen, Eltingen, Ochsenwang, Weilheim and Ötlingen) during which time he performed his duties unenthusiastically and without a sense of vocation. Not until 1834, when he was the oldest curate in Württemberg, was he given his own parish at Cleversulzbach; this long delay in promotion may have been the result of the political activities of his brother Karl, which threw the suspicion of revolutionary sympathies on Eduard also. In February, 1828, he made a bold attempt to escape from duties which had become distasteful to him. In his new post as journalist, however, he was expected to provide copy at regular intervals; such discipline was too irksome and he was pleased to return, after a few months of such 'freedom', to the comparatively easy-going routine of curate.

In 1829 he became engaged to Luise Rau, a clergyman's daughter, in whose love he found inspiration and happiness; they parted in 1833, mainly because of Mörike's unwillingness (in Luise's eyes) to exert himself and make a career in the Church. His novel *Maler Nolten* appeared in 1832.

During the years spent as vicar of Cleversulzbach (1834–43)

[1] Camerer, p. 15.

Mörike lived with his mother and sister Klara. After his mother's death in 1841 he came to rely ever more on Klara, who kept house for him. From 1837 to 1841 he enjoyed a period of friendship and lively correspondence with Hermann Kurz, who was responsible for arranging the poems in the order in which they appeared in the 1838 edition (*Gedichte*, Cotta, Stuttgart and Tübingen): later editions, augmented or revised, were brought out by the same publisher in 1847 (dated 1848), 1856 and 1867. While at Cleversulzbach he found his duties more and more onerous, and frequently asked friends or colleagues to preach in his stead; finally, in 1843, he retired from the Church on the grounds of ill-health after a markedly undistinguished career.

After spending a year divided between Wermutshausen, where he stayed with his friend Hartlaub, and Schwäbisch-Hall, he settled at Mergentheim, where he met his future wife, Gretchen Speeth, marrying her in 1851 and moving to Stuttgart the same year. Gretchen was a Catholic, and many of Mörike's friends, among them his greatest, Hartlaub, caused him pain by expressing open disapproval of the marriage. While living in Stuttgart he gave lectures on German literature or readings from its major works to the girl pupils of the *Katharinenstift*, continuing with these far from burdensome duties until 1867. In 1853 his stories *Das Stuttgarter Hutzelmännlein* and *Die Hand der Jezerte* were published, and in 1855 his *Novelle*, the prose masterpiece *Mozart auf der Reise nach Prag*. His interest in translation found expression in *Klassische Blumenlese* (1840), *Theokritos, Bion und Moschos* (1855, with Friedrich Notter) and *Anakreon und die sogenannten Anakreontischen Lieder* (1864) in which he brought out versions of Greek and Latin poets—often his own versions or his own revision of earlier attempts. Related to this work is his fine *Idylle vom Bodensee* (1846).

The sixteen years in Stuttgart brought Mörike much joy (the birth of his daughters, Fanny, 1855, and Marie, 1857, a visit from Theodor Storm, and periods of friendship with Paul Heyse and Moritz von Schwind), but with the passing of time it became obvious that the rival and enmity between Gretchen and Klara, which caused him great unhappiness, would endure as long as they lived together. In his last years he left his wife, and moved from place to place (Bebenhausen, Lorch, Stuttgart, Nürtingen). Husband and wife were reconciled shortly before Mörike's death (June 4, 1875).

During the course of his life Mörike frequently complained of ill-health; one cannot avoid the suspicion that some of this was imagined and that he was a hypochondriac who used what he regarded as his delicate state of health to escape irksome tasks. There can be little doubt that he disliked all forms of work which involved regular application. On the other hand, he was ready to devote both time and energy to hobbies and interests such as pets (he was fond of birds and animals), drawing and painting, some examples of which underline his abnormality and taste for the macabre or grotesque, pottery and the composition of occasional poems. He was temperamental, often childish, in his behaviour and kept only the most patient and understanding of his friends, Hartlaub, as a companion for life, eventually breaking off relations with all the others for long periods as a result of some difference of opinion. His laziness induced him to delay replying to letters until he had often offended his correspondent. On the basis of what is known of Mörike's life, August Müller[1] has described him in medical terms as 'einen einseitig dichterisch stark, sonst aber schwach begabten Psychopathen', a judicious summing-up in which the key word is 'einseitig', for Mörike, a failure in almost all other respects, was a great poet. His existence, burdened by the 'common round', real or imagined ill-health and an inability to solve everyday problems, was lived out within a narrowly restricted geographical area; it stands in striking contrast to the profound spiritual and emotional experience reflected in his poetry. Yet his poems do not arise from any conflict in him between the real and the ideal; as long as he could dream and see visions, he was undisturbed by the meanness or pettiness of his environment, he was able indeed to transfigure it through his poetic fancy. Since he found the world of everyday either insufficient or frightening, and since he soon discovered that he could never fully belong to the world of nature in which there were mysteries unfathomable to humans, he sought a personal compromise in the creation of a fantastic and delightful no man's land spanning the two worlds. One of the best examples is the legend of Orplid, which we must examine in more detail when we consider the poet's originality.

Out of touch and out of sympathy with the main stream of contemporary literature in which questions of the day, both social and political, were the favourite themes, Mörike neverthe-

[1] August Müller, p. 91.

less occupied a central position among Swabian poets and writers through his friendship with Kerner, Vischer, Strauß, Hartlaub, Kurz and others. However, all these men, although undoubtedly gifted, stood far below him in the field of literature (the difference between talent and genius). They rarely understood his eminence or the quality of his genius, e.g. Vischer censured what he called the fantastic element in his poetry, and he and Strauß constantly urged him to compose a drama, a historical novel, or some kind of work involving the study of history.[1]

Most of Mörike's work owed little to the views or example of his contemporaries, for he turned for inspiration to inherited riches, the poetry of classical literatures, the *Volkslied*, the works of Schiller and, above all, Goethe, of whom he sometimes spoke as the father-poet (*Dichtervater*). *Wilhelm Meisters Lehrjahre* and the Goethe-Schiller correspondence were among his favourite reading. The themes he selected were unrelated to the political events of his time, indeed his output declined visibly in the years around 1848. An examination of the dates of composition of his collected poems reveals that he enjoyed three main peaks of production in the years 1827–8, 1837–8 and 1845–6, at the age of 23–4, 33–4, and 41–2, while he wrote only a handful of poems in each of the other years of composition. These periods of peak production do not correspond in time to focal points in his own life, as they do for Annette von Droste-Hülshoff.[2] Mörike had the great gift of patience, the secret of allowing his personal experience to mature, so that it could be expressed in terms of universal significance. It is this quality above all which brings him close to his revered predecessor and raises him above such post-Goethean poets as Eichendorff and Lenau. As he wrote to Kurz in 1838,[3] he considered it essential to await a suitable mood ('die Stimmung abwarten') before composing. One of his favourite sayings was 'no nix forciere'.[4]

Storm relates that Mörike said of poetic creation: 'es müsse nur so viel sein, daß man eine Spur von sich zurücklasse, die Hauptsache aber sei das Leben selbst, das man darüber nicht

---

[1] Robert Vischer, pp. 146 (1/4/1838), 106 (22/10/1833), Strauß (3), p. 54.
[2] Annette von Droste-Hülshoff, *Sämtliche Werke* (ed. C. Heselhaus), Carl Hanser, Munich, 1952, p. 1044.
[3] Kindermann, p. 148.
[4] See Goes, (2) [1944] p. 60.

vergessen dürfe'.[1] By 'Leben' he means of course the personal life of the individual, not social or political events; something of the poet's being must be incorporated in his work, a trace of his personality which will survive his physical death. As a poet Mörike profited from those very characteristics which made him seem unreliable, sluggish and ineffective as a man, passivity and receptivity of impressions and emotions. Although some of his poems were filed with care when he was dissatisfied with the original form, others arose directly from moments of inspiration and vision. The essence of such subtle impressions is, however, preserved and conveyed in the poems through Mörike's mastery of form, his ability to express the desired shade of meaning in a verse-form attuned to it.

Among the outstanding qualities of his poetry are music and subtlety (even irregularity) of rhythm. Mörike was intensely moved by music[2] and possessed a fine sense of rhythm. Writing of prosody W. P. Ker[3] speaks of the 'shadowy bodiless music in the mind of the poet before the poem is made' and stresses the intimate relationship between content and form ('the form does not remain an external or mechanical frame; it is adopted by the mind, in the same sort of way as a dance tune becomes the rhythm of the dancers'). That Mörike understood the fundamental significance of the relationship between form and content, especially for the criterion of beauty in art, may be seen from the following remarks in a letter to Ostertag of 1838[4] (translated by the present writer):

> In its most profound sense form is . . . absolutely inseparable from content, indeed almost one with it in its origin, and something completely incorporeal and extremely fragile. I do not insist on conformity to the rules as long as there is *beauty*. A beautiful thought or emotion can only become manifest in poetry through beauty of form, without it a beautiful thought or vision has actually no value from the point of view of art. The form must therefore be as perfect as possible. In my opinion the form also determines the success of the poet, I mean the approval of his readers; this is right and proper, for fine thoughts, charming pictures, wit, etc., others can possess, but it is the merit of the poet that he can provide us with all these things and win our hearts by means of a form which is solidly complete and harmonious; this is decisive in all essentials for his character and the value of his work for all time.

As this passage would suggest, Mörike was a seeker after

---

[1] Storm, p. 31.
[2] See note on poem 'An Wilhelm Hartlaub'.
[3] W. P. Ker, *Form and Style in Poetry*, London, 1929, pp. 95, 100.
[4] Rath (4), pp. 50-1.

beauty; this he often found in things and places remote from the bustle of life ('Auf eine Lampe', 'Die schöne Buche', 'Bilder aus Bebenhausen'). A work of art, he maintained, writing in December, 1831,[1] should make the reader feel 'zu allem Schönen aufgelegt'; *Wilhelm Meister* and the works of Homer evoke this mood in him.

Like Goethe, Mörike was a *Gelegenheitsdichter* in the best sense, composing when inspired by an occasion or experience, not to order; he must have read with approval Goethe's remark in a letter to Schiller dated December 27, 1797:[2]

> Leider werden wir Neuern wohl auch gelegentlich als Dichter geboren, und wir plagen uns in der ganzen Gattung herum, ohne recht zu wissen, woran wir eigentlich sind, denn die spezifischen Bestimmungen sollten . . . eigentlich von außen kommen und die Gelegenheit das Talent determinieren.

In a letter to Waiblinger dated 1821[3] Mörike wrote enthusiastically of Goethe's *Dichtung und Wahrheit*; inspired by not only its beauty, but also its humanity, he was delighted to perceive in it the human qualities of its author. He was clearly interested in the role of the author's personality in a work and had no taste or talent for reflective poetry like that of Schiller. At the same time philosophy, which attracted his friends and indeed most German poets as a field of study, meant little to him as compared with poetry; he was at one with Schiller in the view that he expressed in a letter to Goethe[4] 'der Dichter ist der einzige wahre Mensch, und der beste Philosoph ist nur eine Karikatur gegen ihn'. Mörike valued the beauty that he saw in life higher than philosophy, knowing that recourse to the latter can never compensate for loss of the former. Writing to Strauß,[5] he asked for the original English text of Romeo's answer when the Friar tries to console him with philosophy for the separation from Juliet; Mörike wants the words for a motto. Romeo's famous reply runs: 'Hang up philosophy! / Unless philosophy can make a Juliet'.

Mörike's poems are the products of unreflective and often incredibly naive genius, many of them appearing superficial and devoid of serious thought at a first reading. The poetic achievement in these can only be appreciated through a closer

---

[1] Rath (3), p. 208.
[2] Goethe, *Gedenkausgabe der Werke, Briefe und Gespräche*, Zürich, 1949, XX, 1, p. 478.
[3] Seebaß (1), p. 9.
[4] Goethe, *op. cit.*, p. 55 (7/1/1795).
[5] Walter, p. 594 (5/2/1838).

B

study of the text and an absorption of unforgettably striking lines like 'Er fühlt mir schon herauf die Brust, / Er kühlt mit Liebesschauerlust' ('Mein Fluß') or 'Glänzet empor ein Hahnenschrei' ('Der alte Turmhahn') or 'O holde Nacht, du gehst mit leisem Tritt / Auf schwarzem Samt, der nur am Tage grünet' ('Gesang zu zweien in der Nacht'). In addition there are about a dozen poems which are written at a different, more profound level, and bear witness to Mörike's awareness of the tragic aspects of human existence; 'Zitronenfalter im April', 'Denk' es, o Seele!', 'Der Feuerreiter' and 'Erinna an Sappho' are examples of these. Nietzsche was guilty of short-sightedness and prejudice when he noted in 1875:[1]

Ich sah mir darauf diesen Mörike wieder an und fand ihn, mit Ausnahme von vier bis fünf Sachen in der deutschen Volksliedmanier, ganz schwach und undichterisch. Vor allem fehlt es ganz an Klarheit der Anschauung . . . so ein süßlich-weichliches Schwimm-schwimm und Klingkling . . . Knaben-Unbestimmtheit des Gefühls.

Even in the poems of his youth, which tend towards *Stimmungslyrik* or the evocation of atmosphere or mood, Mörike succeeded in portraying the most elusive emotions with almost unprecedented clarity; in his later poetry it is possible to trace a shift of emphasis towards the *Dinggedicht* or the poem imbued with the spirit of Greek or Latin literature—here again the presentation is abnormally lucid. The accusation that his work lacks 'Klarheit der Anschauung' is certainly unjust.

The characteristics of the swiftly developing poet, in particular those of a visionary, are well described by Hermann Hesse,[2] one of the most perceptive of Mörike's readers:

Dem etwa Zwanzigjährigen, den seine Freunde einer unerschöpflich frohsprudelnden Laune wegen liebten, begegnete es nicht selten, daß in frohen, guten Augenblicken ihm plötzlich die ganze Umgebung zu einem verzauberten Bilde erstarrte, in dem er mit staunenden Augen stand und die rätselhafte Schönheit der Welt wie eine Mahnung und beinahe wie einen feinen, heimlichen Schmerz sah.

As may be seen from a number of poems, in particular 'An einem Wintermorgen vor Sonnenaufgang', Mörike's awareness and insight were peculiarly sharpened at moments of transition from night to day or during the night itself. Night and day are certainly contrasted, day sometimes being viewed as a point of hope after a sleepless night ('In der Frühe'), sometimes as a time

---

[1] Nietzsche, *Werke*, Leipzig, 1903, x, Zweite Abtheilung, p.490, 'Aus dem Jahre 1875'.

[2] Hesse, *Fabulierbuch*, Fritz und Wasmuth Verlag A.G. Zurich, n.d., p. 304.

whose worldly bustle interferes with the poet's communion with Nature ('der freche Tag' in 'Gesang zu zweien in der Nacht'). This ambivalence springs from Mörike's own hesitation between the choice of human companionship[1] and that of communion with Nature in the uncertain hope of penetrating its secrets, yet this rarely develops to a conflict such as Faust must endure from the 'two souls' in his breast, principally because of a palliative—Mörike's own world of fantasy.

To understand Mörike the poet it is essential to consider his attitude to the hereafter; this was conditioned by the interest he shared with Justinus Kerner in spirits, inexplicable phenomena and the occult. Mörike's beliefs, which corresponded in general to some ideas expressed by one of the few philosophers who influenced him, Schelling, cannot be called a philosophy in the stricter sense. He accepted the Romantic teachings of *Magischer Idealismus* that nothing in Nature was dead, no material form without soul and life, that all things were linked in a system of elective affinities which worked through *Sympathie*. Because he has fallen into sin, Mörike would argue, Man has caused his own failure to perceive this truth, and has abandoned intuition for rational belief. The transcendental, normally hidden from Man, is experienced by him in the transition from sleep to waking—hence the importance of somnolence for Mörike. In *Maler Nolten* he formulates his own pantheistic belief 'daß hinter jedem sichtbaren Dinge, es sei dies, was es wolle — ein Holz, ein Stein oder der Hahn und Knopf auf dem Turme — ein Unsichtbares, hinter jeder toten Sache ein geistiges Etwas steckt'.[2] God, he thought, could not be conjured up, but came uncalled; hence he found it impossible to reconcile his own views of the Deity with those of the Church: in his sermons and, in a playful, semi-ironic manner, in his poems, he represents God as the patriarchal father. He always regarded the destructive aspects of death with horror (here his reaction is very similar to that of the Greeks) and yet he kept a firm belief in an after-life. In 1865 Theodor Storm expressed his regret in a letter to Mörike that he could not share his friend's 'glücklichen Glauben'.[3]

[1] Mörike was a social being, yet clearly hated certain aspects of society—thus in 'Am Walde' he finds comfort in the forest; 'Da ist mir wohl, und meine schlimmste Plage, / Den Fratzen der Gesellschaft mich zu fügen, / Hier wird sie mich doch endlich nicht bekriegen, / Wo ich auf eigne Weise mich behage.'

[2] *Maler Nolten* (1832), Baumann, II, p. 267.

[3] Rath (2), p. 111.

After the death of his mother in 1841 Mörike wrote to Hemsen 'daß es nichts Gewisseres für mich gibt, als unsere jenseitige Fortdauer, und daß sich diese Überzeugung mir seit Jahren unwiderstehlich auf einem Gebiet der Erfahrung aufdrang, von welchem die Wissenschaft leider bis jetzt noch allzu selten Notiz genommen hat'.[1] Here he links his interest in the occult with his belief in the hereafter.

Mörike's behaviour in marrying a Catholic and making friends with the Catholic clergy or attending Catholic services seems at first sight very strange for a Protestant clergyman, but it would be wrong to infer from it that he was in sympathy with the teachings of the Church of Rome. However, there can be no doubt that he was exceptionally tolerant in religious questions and that the aesthetic aspect of Roman Catholicism appealed to his sense of beauty.

One of Mörike's most striking gifts is his originality; although he may draw inspiration from the work of others, he rarely makes use of a story at second hand, preferring to invent his own mythology. This process began through a poetic game of make-believe in Tübingen, to which the shadow-play 'Der letzte König von Orplid'[2] in *Maler Nolten* owes its origin. His friend Bauer also composed two plays 'Der heimliche Maluff' and 'Orplids letzte Tage' which are products of the preoccupation with the mythology of Orplid, but these are artistically inferior to Mörike's play. Orplid, originally conceived as an extension of the topography in the Tübingen district including the Neckar, was finally imagined as an island somewhere in the Pacific between New Zealand and South America. The native goddess of the place was called Weyla, and she gave her name to the river on the island (based on the Neckar). The beautiful poem 'Gesang Weylas' was probably written in 1831, and presents Orplid in its golden age:

> Du bist Orplid, mein Land!
> Das ferne leuchtet;
> Vom Meere dampfet dein besonnter Strand
> Den Nebel, so der Götter Wange feuchtet.
>
> Uralte Wasser steigen
> Verjüngt um deine Hüften, Kind!
> Vor deiner Gottheit beugen
> Sich Könige, die deine Wärter sind.

[1] Seebaß (1), p. xx.
[2] See Baumann, II, pp. 100-37 (1832 version) and 495-519 (revised version).

Mörike's play is concerned with a much later period in its imagined history when the race of heroes on the island has long since incurred the anger of the gods and been swept away; all that remains of their life and civilization some thousand years after its time of prosperity is the ruins of the town and castle of Orplid and a single member of the race, the tragic King Ulmon, who, as a result of Weyla's protection, survived the general destruction and lived on, passed over by death. Meanwhile, some Europeans have come upon the island by chance and established a small colony there which, however, lacks the knowledge, culture and poetry of the original Orplid civilization of which Ulmon is the only survivor. Ulmon is being tested by the gods to prove himself worthy of divinity; he longs for death and for escape from the enchantment which draws him, even against his will, to the fairy Thereile who loves him. With the help of the judge Kollmer, Ulmon secures possession of an old book from which he learns how to break Thereile's power over him; he is now free to die and be gathered to the gods. Two of the poet's comic figures, the 'Buchdrucker' and Wispel, are introduced as the finders of the mysterious book, while a number of fairy children appear as Thereile's subordinates. The gulf separating mortal and fairy is stressed in the love-hate relationship of Ulmon and Thereile and in the homelessness of Silpelitt who is half fairy, half mortal and fully at home in neither sphere. The poetic beauty of the legend is exemplified in the strange prophecy of how Ulmon will be released from his torment:

> Ein Mensch lebt seiner Jahre Zahl,
> Ulmon allein wird sehen
> Den Sommer kommen und gehen
> Zehnhundertmal.

> Einst eine schwarze Weide blüht,
> Ein Kindlein muß sie fällen,
> Dann rauschen die Todeswellen,
> Drin Ulmons Herz verglüht.

> Auf Weylas Mondenstrahl
> Sich Ulmon soll erheben,
> Sein Götterleib dann schweben
> Zum blauen Saal.

Like the poet himself Ulmon moves in two worlds, that of the society of his day (here the settlers through his contact with Kollmer) and that of Nature (the fairies) without being fully at home in either; he is tormented by existence and enchanted by certain aspects of Nature which enslave him (Thereile), he is not a late-comer, but, like the late-comer Mörike, he is out of sympathy with his own age and looks to a past of greater cultural wealth for inspiration.

One facet of the poet's gift of originality found expression in the jokes that Mörike shared with his friends, 'Der sichere Mann' resulting from one of these; such creations, the fruits of his absorption in Nature and of the profound influence of classical literatures, often reveal his love for the grotesque and even the macabre.

In *Maler Nolten* Mörike wrote of Jung Volker,[1] 'Sein Innres bespiegelte die Welt wie die Sonne einen Becher goldnen Weines', a description peculiarly apposite to the poet's own genius for poetic and humorous invention. It is often asserted that German literature is deficient in humorous writing, but perhaps it would be more fair to say that there is a lack of humorous writing which appeals to British tastes. Mörike's humorous poetry, of which only a small quantity can be included in this selection, is amusing, even to the foreign reader. Although often intensely whimsical, his humour is as important for an understanding of the poet as his views on the universe or human life. Originating in his highly imaginative sense of fun, his humorous poetry often contains self-mockery. Criticism of the foibles of others is directed against types rather than personalities, e.g. in 'An Longus' and only becomes bitter when he is attacking affectation or insincerity. In 'Erbauliche Betrachtung' he addresses his own feet, in 'Waldplage' he is plagued by midges while reading Klopstock in the forest, in 'Der alte Turmhahn' the church weathercock is brought to life to comment on the parson and his home, in 'Häusliche Szene' schoolmaster and spouse discuss in elegiac couplets a domestic problem. This aspect of Mörike's work was understood and loved by his contemporaries, and was largely responsible for the once popular view that he was an idyllic poet enjoying the carefree tranquillity of a Philistine existence; at this level he seems to fit well enough into the Swabian literary scene in which eccentricity and humorous fantasy are not uncommon (cf. Kerner or F. Th. Vischer).

More astute critics have maintained that Mörike deliberately

---

[1] Baumann, II, p. 284.

cultivated and stressed the idyllic note in his poetry, using it as a mask and safeguard against the storms of passion inherent in life. This view is more perceptive, and is supported by evidence in a number of poems that the poet was only too aware of the dangers of intense emotional experience and of the tragedy of human existence. Vischer in old age finally recognized this trait in the poet and his work, as may be seen from this extract from his speech at the unveiling of a memorial to Mörike in 1880 (he is addressing his dead friend):[1]

Du kennst die Welt der Ängste, die Abgründe in der Seele und die Klüfte des Lebens, du kennst Schauer und Grauen und wüßtest, was Unheimliches die Welt des Verbrechens, der Untreue, des Mords, der Verzweiflung umwittert und umhaucht, doch nie versankst du in dieses Grauen, stets siegte der schöne *Gleichmut* der reingestimmten Seele.

In his early work Mörike seeks to lose himself in Nature and to ignore his inevitable physical death. Later, as the end of his personal life on earth draws nearer, he struggles to reconcile himself to this fact, and to look at the problem objectively (note the change from the subjective approach in 'Denk' es, o Seele!' to the humorously pathetic or almost impartial treatment in 'Besuch in der Kartause' and 'Erinna an Sappho' respectively).

Nature, love and human life are the most important themes in Mörike's poetry; these cannot always be discussed separately, nature and love, for example, are seen in the most intimate relationship one to the other. His devotion to the landscape of Swabia does not cause his work to become narrowly provincial, but deepens its significance for him and his readers. From 'An einem Wintermorgen, vor Sonnenaufgang' and the Orplid poems onwards he experiences moments of tremendous poetic vision; his imaginative powers enable him to transfigure the natural scene into dream landscapes of fantastic beauty, as in the 'Peregrina' cycle. In his love poems the erotic note is seldom absent, yet the sensuality retains a naive, almost innocent quality. That these poems are *Erlebnisdichtung* in the fullest sense cannot be doubted. Human life is represented in ballads and in poems inspired by *Volkslied*, works of art, artists and poets.

Mörike's greatest sources of inspiration were the *Volkslied*, Goethe and the poetry of the ancients. His folk poems were never imitated *Volkslieder*, but original *Kunstlieder* in the *Volkslied* style. Kapff has shown that, in the years 1830-1, he worked

[1] Robert Vischer, p. 312.

long and carefully on a collection of Swabian *Volkslieder*. Kapff has also asserted that the folk poems by Mörike, mainly of the Cleversulzbach period, were based on memories of these earlier studies; it is true that the folk poems were mostly written in the eighteen-thirties, particularly in 1837, and it is probable that the work on Swabian *Volkslieder* was an important, possibly decisive, landmark in this aspect of his poetic development. Many features of the genuine *Volkslied* are to be seen in his poems, including desultory narration, hyperbole, repetition in various forms, archaisms and colloquial expressions, metrical irregularity, impure or dialect (often Swabian) rhymes; most of these, which are examined in detail by Heilmann, could only have been learned from prolonged and intensive study. Here Mörike was following the example of Goethe; he read his correspondence with Schiller in the years 1829 to 1831, and undoubtedly noted Goethe's views on poetic composition, such as this statement (in a letter to Schiller of April 3, 1801)[1] which incidentally defines Mörike's own approach:

> Die Dichtkunst verlangt im Subjekt, das sie ausüben soll, eine gewisse gutmütige, ins Reale verliebte Beschränktheit, hinter welcher das Absolute verborgen liegt. Die Forderungen von oben herein zerstören jenen unschuldigen produktiven Zustand.

The influence of Greek and Latin literature, derived from his early schooling in the classics and his later work as a translator, is seen most clearly in the theme and metre of poems written from the eighteen-thirties onwards.

Mörike's novel *Maler Nolten* (1832) contains fourteen fine poems, many of which are included in this selection. The context in which the poems appear is often of great assistance in providing a relevant explanation of certain points, and for this reason the setting of each poem introduced into the novel has been carefully examined whenever this seems necessary.

Mörike's poetry did not evoke great enthusiasm from the reading public during his lifetime, although its qualities were appreciated by an *élite* which included Storm, Keller, Hebbel, F. Th. Vischer, D. F. Strauß, Mommsen, Burckhardt and Treitschke. According to Maync,[2] it has, however, maintained a steady popularity in musical settings (594 of 123 poems; 83 of 'Das verlassene Mägdlein', 58 of 'Er ist's', 58 of 'Ein Stündlein wohl vor Tag', 57 of 'Schön-Rohtraut', 50 of 'Agnes'). The composers

---

[1] Goethe, *op. cit.*, p. 854.   [2] Maync (2), p. 581.

range from Karl Mörike, Hetsch, Kauffmann, Robert Franz and Silcher to Schumann, Brahms, Hugo Wolf and Distler.

The rich complexity of Mörike's poetry makes an analysis of his poetic development impossible; it can perhaps be argued that his early work shows a romantic approach, his later (after about 1830) an attitude which is akin to that of 'Biedermeier'. The total impression, however, is clearly one of that immense variety in theme and form which caused Hermann Kurz to write to Mörike: 'Sie sind ein poetischer Millionär, dem keine Münze fehlt, außer kupferne'.[1]

[1] Kindermann, p. 43 (23/6/1837).

SELECT BIBLIOGRAPHY

(This includes works referred to in the Introduction and Notes: they are listed in alphabetical order under the abbreviated reference given—usually the name of the author or editor. Where one person has written or edited several works, these have been numbered; both name and number will be given for reference.)

Adorno, Theodor W. 'Rede über Lyrik und Gesellschaft', *Akzente*, No. 1, 1957, pp. 19–22 ('Auf einer Wanderung').

Baechtold, Jacob. Article in *Allgemeine Deutsche Biographie*, XXII (1885), pp. 243–58.

Baumann, Gerhart (ed.) Eduard Mörike, *Sämtliche Werke*, Stuttgart [1954], 2 vols.

Beck, Adolf.
    (1) 'Mörikes Gedicht "An einem Wintermorgen, vor Sonnenaufgang" mit einem Anhang über die Gedichte "Nachts" und "An eine Äolsharfe" ', *Euphorion*, XLVI, 1952, pp. 370–93.
    (2) 'Peregrina. Forschungsbericht', *Euphorion*, XLVII, 1953, pp. 194–217.

Behrend, Fritz (ed.) Eduard Mörike. *Gedichte*, Leipzig, 1928 (facsimile of edition prepared in 1844).

Berger, G. *Mörike und sein Verhältnis zur schwäbischen Romantik*, Kempen in Posen, 1911.

Bithell, Jethro (ed.).
    (1) *An Anthology of German Poetry* 1830–80, Methuen, London, n.d.
    (2) Introduction in *Poems by Eduard Mörike*, translated by Norah K. Cruickshank and Gilbert F. Cunningham, London, 1959.

Blaze, Henri. 'De la Poésie Lyrique en Allemagne. Édouard Moerike', *Revue des Deux Mondes*, III, 1845, pp. 118–28. Review of 1838 edition of poems (in French).

Bock, Emil. *Boten des Geistes*. Schwäbische Geistesgeschichte und christliche Zukunft, 3rd rev. ed. Stuttgart, 1955: incl. 'Mörike — Das Übersinnliche in Ahnung und Erinnerung'.

Burger, Marcella. *Die Gegenständlichkeit in Mörikes lyrischem Verhalten*, Diss. Heidelberg, 1945.

Camerer, W. (ed.) *Briefe von Eduard Mörike, seiner Schwester Luise und einigen seiner Freunde*, Stuttgart, 1908.

Closs, August. *The Genius of the German Lyric*, London, 1938.

Corrodi, Paul. 'Das Urbild von Mörikes Peregrina', *Jahrbuch der Literarischen Vereinigung Winterthur*, 1923.

Dhaleine, Raymond. Mörike. *Poésies (Gedichte)*, Aubier, Editions Montaigne, n.d. Preface and translation, both in French.

Eggert-Windegg, Walther. *Eduard Mörike. Sein Leben und Werk*, 2nd ed. Stuttgart, 1919.

Eigenbrodt, Wolrad. 'Denk' es, o Seele', *Euphorion*, XIV, 1907, pp. 349–54.

Emmel, Hildegard. *Mörikes Peregrinadichtung*, Weimar, 1952.

Emmersleben, August. *Das Schicksal in Mörikes Leben und Dichten*, Diss. Kulmbach, 1931.

Ermatinger, Emil. *Die deutsche Lyrik seit Herder*, Leipzig/Berlin, 1925, 3 vols. Mörike in II, pp. 193–215.

Farrell, R. B. 'Mörike's Classical Verse', *Publications of the English Goethe Society*, New Series XXV, 1955–6, pp. 41–62.

Feise, Ernst. 'Eduard Mörike's "Denk' es, o Seele"', *Modern Language Notes*, LXVIII, 1953, pp. 344–7.

Fischer, Hermann. *Eduard Mörike*, Stuttgart, 1881.

Fischer, Karl.

    (1) *Eduard Mörikes Leben und Werke*, Berlin, 1901.

    (2) 'Eduard Mörikes Peregrina und ihr Urbild', Feuilleton, *Frankfurter Zeitung*, Feb. 5, 1902.

    (3) *Eduard Mörikes künstlerisches Schaffen und dichterische Schöpfungen*, Berlin, 1903.

    (4) (ed. with Rudolf Krauß) *Eduard Mörikes Briefe*, Berlin, 1903–4, 2 vols.

Flad, Eugen. *Eduard Mörike und die Antike*, Diss. Münster, 1916.

Gabetti, G. *Lenau e Mörike*, Rome, 1927 (in Italian).

Göpfert, Herbert G. (ed.) *Mörikes sämtliche Werke*. Nachwort von Georg Britting, Hanser, Munich [1954].

Goes, Albrecht.

    (1) ('Um Mitternacht'), *Die neue Rundschau*, XLIX/2, 1938, pp. 162–90.

    (2) *Mörike* (in series 'Die Dichter der Deutschen'), Stuttgart [1944]. New edition (1954).

    (3) *Freude am Gedicht*, Frankfurt a. M., 1952 ('Früh im Wagen', pp. 7–11).

    (4) 'Eduard Mörike', *Die großen Deutschen*, III, Berlin [1956], pp. 284–92.

Graham, Ilse Appelbaum. 'Zu Mörikes Gedicht "Auf eine Lampe" ', *Modern Language Notes*, LXVIII, 1953, pp. 328–33.

Grenzmann, W. *Wege zum Gedicht*, ed. P. Hirschenauer and A. Weber, Munich, 1956, pp. 233–6 (analysis of 'Gesang zu zweien in der Nacht').

Guardini, Romano. *Gegenwart und Geheimnis*, Würzburg, 1957. Includes analyses of 'Die schöne Buche' (see also von Wiese (2) II, pp. 71–8), 'Auf eine Lampe', 'Erinna an Sappho' and 'Märchen vom sichern Mann'.

Günthert, Julius Ernst von. *Mörike und Notter*, Berlin/Stuttgart, 1895.

Gundolf, Friedrich. *Romantiker*, Neue Folge, Berlin, 1931. Mörike, pp. 218–53.

Hartlaub, Gustav F. 'Eduard Mörike und der "Sehrmann" ', *Euphorion*, XLVI, 1952, pp. 80–4.

Heilmann, Daniel Friedrich. *Mörikes Lyrik und das Volkslied*; Berliner Beiträge zur germ. und roman. Philologie, ed. Emil Ebering, XLVII, Germanistische Abteilung 34, Berlin, 1913. The most useful work on this aspect.

Heinsius, Walter. 'Mörike und die Romantik', *Deutsche Vierteljahrsschrift*, III, 1925, pp. 194–230.

Heiseler, Bernt v. 'Mörikes Vers', *Ahnung und Aussage*, Gütersloh [1952], pp. 42–9.

Hesse, Hermann (ed.). *Deutsche Lyriker* VIII. *Eduard Mörike*, Leipzig, n.d. Short selection of poems with introduction.

Heyse, Paul. *Literaturblatt des Deutschen Kunstblattes*, I, 1845. Essay on Mörike.

Hieber, Hermann. *Mörikes Gedankenwelt*, Stuttgart, 1923.

Hirsch, K.

(1) 'Bemerkungen zu Mörikes Elegie "An eine Äolsharfe" ', *Literarische Beilage des Staats-Anzeigers für Württemberg*, 1912, pp. 103–6.

(2) 'Zur Entstehung von Mörikes Äolsharfe', ditto, 1914, pp. 25–7.

(3) 'Das Urbild von Mörikes "Prior der Kartause" ', ditto, 1920, pp. 186–93.

(4) 'Mörikes Kartause und das Kloster Ittingen', ditto, 1921, pp. 18–21.

(5) 'Zur Geschichte der Mörikischen Orpliddichtung', ditto, 1922, pp. 249–64.

Hoffmeister, Johannes (ed.). *Nachgoethesche Lyrik. Eichendorff/Lenau/Mörike*, Bonn, 1948. Valuable introduction.

Ibel, Rudolf. *Weltschau deutscher Dichter*, Hamburg, 1948 (Mörike, pp. 185–268).

Ilgenstein, Heinrich. *Mörike und Goethe*, Berlin, 1902.

Jacob, Kurt. *Aufbau und innere Gestaltung der Balladen und anderer Gedichte Mörikes*, Diss. Frankfurt a.M., 1934.

Kaiser, Franz. *Die antiken Versmaße Mörikes*, Diss. Tübingen, 1923.

Kapff, Rudolf. 'Mörike und das schwäbische Volkslied', *Literarische Beilage des Staats-Anzeigers für Württemberg*, 1919, pp. 213–16.

Kempski, Jürgen v. 'Zu Mörikes "Denk' es, o Seele" ', *Merkur*, I, 1947, pp. 475–7.

Kindermann, Heinz (ed.). *Briefwechsel zwischen Hermann Kurz und Eduard Mörike*, Stuttgart, 1919.

Klaiber, J. *Eduard Mörike. Zwei Vorträge*, Stuttgart, 1876.

Klein, J. *Geschichte der deutschen Lyrik*, Wiesbaden, 1957, pp. 534–48.

Kneisel, Jessie H. *Mörike and Music*, Ph.D. diss., Columbia, 1949.

Kohlschmidt, W. 'Wehmut, Erinnerung, Sehnsucht in Mörikes Gedicht', *Wirkendes Wort*, I, 1950–1, pp. 229–38 (also in *Form und Innerlichkeit*, Bern, 1955, pp. 233–47).

Koschlig, Manfred.

(1) *Mörike in seiner Welt*, Stuttgart, 1954. The poet's story in well produced pictures and photographs.

(2) 'Mörike's *Neujahr* in Ochsenwang', *Stultifera navis*, Jg. 14, no. 1–2, 1957, pp. 89–91.

Krauß, Rudolf.

(1) *Eduard Mörike als Gelegenheitsdichter*, Stuttgart/Leipzig/Berlin/Vienna, 1895.

(2) 'Studien zu Eduard Mörikes Gedichten', *Euphorion*, II, Ergänzungsheft, 1895, pp. 99–121.

(3) (ed.) *Eduard Mörikes sämtliche Werke*, Max Hesse, Leipzig [1911], 6 vols.

See also Karl Fischer (4).

Kuh, Emil. *Kritische und literarhistorische Aufsätze*, ed. Alfred Schaer, Vienna, 1910, pp. 416–54, in *Schriften des Literarischen Vereins in Wien*, XIV, Reviews and articles.

Kunisch, H. *Wege zum Gedicht*, ed. P. Hirschenauer and A. Weber, Munich, 1956, pp. 237–56 (Peregrina poems).

Leffson, August (ed.). *Mörikes Werke*, Bong, Berlin [1908], 4 vols.

Märtens, Ilse. *Die Mythologie bei Mörike*, Diss. Marburg a.d. Lahn, 1921.

Mare, Margaret. *Eduard Mörike*, London, 1957. The only biography in English.

Martini, Fritz. 'Eduard Mörikes Dichtertum', *Der christliche Student*, July, 1950.

Maurer, K.-W. (ed.). *Eduard Mörike. Gedichte*, Duckworth, London, 1947. Introduction in collaboration with Albrecht Goes.

Maync, Harry.
   (1) (ed.) *Mörikes Werke*, Leipzig/Vienna, 2nd ed. [1914], 3 vols.
   (2) *Eduard Mörike*, 5th rev. ed. Stuttgart [1944]. The most reliable and detailed biography.
   (3) 'David Friedrich Strauß und Eduard Mörike', *Deutsche Rundschau*, cxv, pp. 94–117, 1903. Includes 12 unpublished letters.

Meyer, Herbert. *Eduard Mörike*, Stuttgart [1950]. A perceptive study.

Mohrhenn, Alfred. *Lebendige Dichtung*, Heidelberg/Darmstadt, 1956. Essay on Mörike, pp. 30–42.

Müller, August. *Bismarck, Nietzsche, Scheffel, Mörike*, Bonn, 1921.

Müller, Brigitte. *Eduard Mörike. Grundriß seines Dichtertums*, Winterthur, 1955.

Müller, Joachim.
   (1) 'Der Lyriker Eduard Mörike', *Neue Jahrbücher für Wissenschaft und Jugendbildung*, xiii, 1937, pp. 249–62.
   (2) 'An einem Wintermorgen, vor Sonnenaufgang', *Deutsche Vierteljahrsschrift*, xxv, 1951, pp. 82–93.

Mundhenk, Alfred. 'Der umgesattelte Feuerreiter. Eine Studie zu Mörikes Ballade und ihre beiden Fassungen', *Wirkendes Wort*, v, 1954–5, pp. 143–9.

Niebelschütz, Wolf v. *Eduard Mörike*, Bremen, 1948.

Nordheim, Werner v. 'Die Dingdichtung Eduard Mörikes. Erläutert am Beispiel des Gedichtes "Auf eine Lampe"', *Euphorion*, L, 1956, pp. 71–85.

Notter, Friedrich. *Eduard Mörike*, Stuttgart, 1875.

Oppel, Horst. *Peregrina*, Mainz, 1947.

Oppert, Kurt. 'Das Dinggedicht', *Deutsche Vierteljahrsschrift*, IV, 1926, pp. 747–83.

Pfeiffer, Johannes.
(1) 'Über das Erschließen von Gedichten', *Der Deutschunterricht*, No. 3, 1950, pp. 3–23.
(2) *Wege zur Dichtung*, Hamburg, 1954 ('Um Mitternacht', pp. 78–80).

Pollack, H. 'Zur Interpretation von Mörikes Gedicht "Auf eine Lampe" ', *Moderne Språk*, Stockholm, LI, No. 4, pp. 301–5.

Prawer, S. S.
(1) *German Lyric Poetry*. A critical analysis of selected poems from Klopstock to Rilke, London, 1952.
(2) 'Mörike's Second Thoughts', *Modern Philology*, LVII, No. 1, August, 1959.
(3) *Mörike und seine Leser*, Stuttgart, 1960 (Ernst Klett Verlag). The last two of these works had not appeared when the bibliography was closed and have not been seen by the editor.

Proelß, Johannes. 'Hauffs Feuerreuterlied und Mörikes Feuerreiter', *Burschenschaftliche Blätter*, 24 Jg. Nr. 9 ff., Berlin, 1910.

Rahn, Fritz. ('Die traurige Krönung'), *Der Deutschunterricht*, No. 2/3, 1948–9, pp. 55–65.

Rath, Hanns Wolfgang.
(1) (ed.) *Briefwechsel zwischen Eduard Mörike und Moriz Schwind*, Stuttgart [1914].
(2) (ed.) *Briefwechsel zwischen Theodor Storm und Eduard Mörike*, Stuttgart [1919].
(3) (ed.) *Luise. Briefe der Liebe an seine Braut Luise Rau, geschrieben von Eduard Mörike*, in *Schriften der Gesellschaft der Mörikefreunde*, I, 1921.
(4) *Mörikes Epistel an Longus und ihre komi-tragische Vorgeschichte*, in *Schriften der Gesellschaft der Mörikefreunde*, IV, 1924.

Reinhardt, Heinrich. *Mörike und sein Roman Maler Nolten*, Horgen-Zürich/Leipzig, 1930. *Wege der Dichtung*, IX.

Rinhardt, C. (Reinhold Köstlin). 'Die schwäbische Dichterschule und Eduard Mörike', *Hallische Jahrbücher für deutsche Wissenchaft und Kunst*, 1839, Nr. 6–8, pp. 18–19. Interesting judgements by a contemporary.

Reitmeyer, Elisabeth. *Studien zum Problem der Gedichtsammlung*, Diss. Bern/Leipzig, 1935.

Renz, Gotthilf (ed.) *Freundeslieb' und Treu*. 250 *Briefe Eduard Mörikes an Wilhelm Hartlaub*, Leipzig, 1938.

Reuschle, Max. *Die Gestalt der Gedichtsammlung Mörikes*, Diss. Tübingen, 1922.

Sandomirsky, Vera. *Eduard Mörike. Sein Verhältnis zum Biedermeier*. Diss. Erlangen, 1935.

Schaeffer, Albrecht. 'Über Mörike', *Dichter und Dichtung*, Leipzig, 1923, pp. 48–82 ('Früh im Wagen').

Schneider, Wilhelm. *Liebe zum deutschen Gedicht*, Freiburg i. Br., 1952. Includes interpretations of 'Gesang zu zweien in der Nacht' (see also *Gedicht und Gedanke*, ed. Heinz Otto Burger, Halle (Saale), 1942, pp. 244–53), 'Das verlassene Mägdlein', 'Auf eine Lampe', 'Märchen vom sichern Mann'.

Schröder, Hans Eggert. *Mörike. Ein Meister des Lebens*, Berlin, 1936.

Schröder, Rudolf Alexander. *Meister der Sprache*, Witten, 1953.

Schütze, Gertrud. *Mörikes Lyrik und die Überwindung der Romantik*, Diss. Münster, 1940.

Schuster, Mauriz. 'Mörikes Verhältnis zu Horaz und Tibull', *Bayerische Blätter für das Gymnasial-Schulwesen*, 65 Jg. (1929), pp. 220–40.

Schwarz, G. 'Mörikes Lyrik', *Welt und Wort*, Nr. 5, 1948.

Seebaß, F. (ed.).
(1) *Briefe von Eduard Mörike*, Tübingen [1939].
(2) *Mörike. Unveröffentlichte Briefe*, 2nd ed. Stuttgart, 1945. Includes valuable introduction.

Sengle, Friedrich. 'Mörike-Probleme. Auseinandersetzung mit der neuesten Mörike-Literatur (1945–50)', *Germanisch-Romanische Monatsschrift*, XXXIII, 1952, pp. 36–47. Indispensable survey of recent studies and work which still requires to be done.

Slessarev, Helga. *Die Zeit als Element der poetischen Intuition bei Eduard Mörike*, Ph.D. diss. Univ. of Cincinnati, 1955.

Spitzer, Leo. 'Wiederum Mörikes Gedicht "Auf eine Lampe" ', *Trivium*, IX, 1951, pp. 133–47.

Stählin, Friedrich. ('Die traurige Krönung'), *Zeitschrift für Deutschkunde*, L, 1956, pp. 719–23.

Stahlmann, H. 'Das Elfenlied von Mörike', *Wirkendes Wort*, I, 1950–1, pp. 280–2.

Staiger, Emil.
(1) 'Das verlassene Mägdlein', *Trivium*, V, 1947, pp. 45–52.

(2) 'Die Kunst der Interpretation', *Neophilologus*, xxxv, 1951, pp. 1–15 ('Auf eine Lampe').

(3) 'Zu einem Vers von Mörike. Ein Briefwechsel mit Martin Heidegger', *Trivium*, ix, 1951, pp. 1–16 (meaning of last line in 'Auf eine Lampe').

All three articles reprinted in Staiger's *Die Kunst der Interpretation*, Zürich, 1955.

(4) *Grundbegriffe der Poetik* [Zürich], 1946.

Steigerthal, H. J. ' "Am Rheinfall" (in der Unterprima)', *Wirkendes Wort*, March, 1957, No. 3, pp. 173–77.

Stein, Ernst. 'Zur Erschließung der künstlerischen Form lyrischer Gedichte', *Der Deutschunterricht*, 1951, No. 6, pp. 9–16 ('In der Frühe').

Steinberg, S. H. (ed.). *Fifteen German Poets*, Macmillan, London, 1956.

Stemplinger, Eduard. *Die Ewigkeit der Antike*, Leipzig, 1924, pp. 85–96.

Storm, Theodor. 'Meine Erinnerungen an Eduard Mörike', *Werke*, ed. Albert Koester, viii, Insel, Leipzig, 1923, pp. 19–36.

Storz, Gerhard. 'Auf eine Christblume' in *Die deutsche Lyrik*, ed. von Wiese, ii, pp. 79–90. See von Wiese (2).

Strauß, D. F.

(1) *Augsburger Allgemeine Zeitung*, Dec. 4, 1847; review of 1848 edition of poems.

(2) *Kleine Schriften*, Leipzig, 1862, pp. 250 ff.

(3) *Ausgewählte Briefe*, ed. Ed. Zeller, Bonn, 1895.

Taraba, Wolfgang.

(1) *Vergangenheit und Gegenwart bei Eduard Mörike*, Diss. Münster, 1953.

(2) 'Erinna an Sappho' and 'Denk' es, o Seele' in *Die deutsche Lyrik*, ed. von Wiese, ii, pp. 98–101 and 91–7. See von Wiese (2).

Thiele, H. ' "An eine Äolsharfe". Zu dem Gedicht von Eduard Mörike', *Wirkendes Wort*, viii, No. 2, pp. 109–112.

Thomas, L. H. C. 'Eduard Mörike: "Bilder aus Bebenhausen" ', *Modern Language Review*, lv, 1960 (a short article, as yet unpublished).

Trümpler, Ernst. *Mörike und die vier Elemente* (Diss., Zürich), St. Gallen, 1954.

Tschirch, Fritz. ('In der Frühe'), *Der Deutschunterricht*, No. 2/3, 1948–9, pp. 65–73.

Vetter, H. *Mörike und die Romantik* (Diss., Bern), Vienna, 1926.

Vischer, F. T. *Kritische Gänge*, ed. Robert Vischer, 2nd ed. Munich, n.d. II, pp. 20–49. Review of 1838 edition of poems.

Vischer, Robert (ed.) *Briefwechsel zwischen Eduard Mörike und Friedrich Theodor Vischer*, Munich, 1926.

Walder, Hans.
(1) *Mörike und die Romantik*. Diss., Bern, 1920.
(2) *Mörikes Weltanschauung*, Zürich, 1922.

Walter, Karl. 'Ungedruckte Briefe Mörikes an David Friedrich Strauß', *Das literarische Echo*, XXIV, 1921–2, pp. 591–8.

Weischedel, Wilhelm (ed.) *Mörikes Gedichte*, Recklingshausen, 1949.

Weißer, Erich. ('Um Mitternacht'), *Wirkendes Wort*, II/5, June 1952, pp. 289–94.

Wesle, C. 'Mörike der junge Dichter', *Festschrift A. Leitzmann*, Jena, 1937.

Wiese, Benno von.
(1) *Eduard Mörike*, Tübingen/Stuttgart [1950]. A sensitive interpretation of various aspects of Mörike's work.
(2) (ed.) *Die deutsche Lyrik*, Düsseldorf [1957], 2 vols.

Williams, W. D. 'Day and Night Symbolism in some Poems of Mörike', *The Era of Goethe. Essays presented to James Boyd*, Oxford, 1959, pp. 163–78. (Considers 'Gesang zu zweien in der Nacht', 'An einem Wintermorgen . . . ', 'Nachts', 'Um Mitternacht', 'In der Frühe'.) Unfortunately this scholarly essay only appeared after the edition had been completed.

Woodtli-Löffler, Susi. ' "Windebang". Die Bedeutung des Windes bei Eduard Mörike', *Trivium*, III, 1945, pp. 198–217.

Wooley, E. O. 'Du bist Orplid, mein Land', *Monatshefte*, XL, 1948, pp. 137–48.

Zemp, Werner.
(1) Mörike, *Elemente und Anfänge*, Frauenfeld/Leipzig, 1939 in *Wege zur Dichtung*, ed. Emil Ermatinger, XXXIII, 1939.
(2) (ed.) Nachwort in *Mörike: Gedichte und Erzählungen*, Manesse, Zürich, 1945, pp. 509–68.
(3) 'Eduard Mörike', *Neue Zürcher Zeitung*, Sept. 4, 1954, Nr. 243, Blatt 4.

EDUARD MÖRIKE POEMS

1. DER FEUERREITER

Sehet ihr am Fensterlein
Dort die rote Mütze wieder?
Nicht geheuer muß es sein,
Denn er geht schon auf und nieder.
5 Und auf einmal welch Gewühle
Bei der Brücke, nach dem Feld!
Horch! das Feuerglöcklein gellt:
       Hinterm Berg,
       Hinterm Berg
10 Brennt es in der Mühle!

Schaut! da sprengt er wütend schier
Durch das Tor, der Feuerreiter,
Auf dem rippendürren Tier,
Als auf einer Feuerleiter!
15 Querfeldein! Durch Qualm und Schwüle
Rennt er schon und ist am Ort!
Drüben schallt es fort und fort:
       Hinterm Berg,
       Hinterm Berg
20 Brennt es in der Mühle!

Der so oft den roten Hahn
Meilenweit von fern gerochen,
Mit des heil'gen Kreuzes Span
Freventlich die Glut besprochen —
25 Weh! dir grinst vom Dachgestühle
Dort der Feind im Höllenschein.
Gnade Gott der Seele dein!
       Hinterm Berg,
       Hinterm Berg
30 Rast er in der Mühle!

Keine Stunde hielt es an,
Bis die Mühle borst in Trümmer:
Doch den kecken Reitersmann
Sah man von der Stunde nimmer.
35 Volk und Wagen im Gewühle
Kehren heim von all dem Graus;
Auch das Glöcklein klinget aus:
        Hinterm Berg,
        Hinterm Berg
40 Brennt's —

Nach der Zeit ein Müller fand
Ein Gerippe samt der Mützen
Aufrecht an der Kellerwand
Auf der beinern Mähre sitzen:
45 Feuerreiter, wie so kühle
Reitest du in deinem Grab!
Husch! da fällt's in Asche ab.
        Ruhe wohl,
        Ruhe wohl
50 Drunten in der Mühle!

2. PEREGRINA

(Aus: „Maler Nolten")

I

Der Spiegel dieser treuen, braunen Augen
Ist wie von innerm Gold ein Widerschein;
Tief aus dem Busen scheint er's anzusaugen,
Dort mag solch Gold in heil'gem Gram gedeihn.
5 In diese Nacht des Blickes mich zu tauchen,
Unwissend Kind, du selber lädst mich ein —
Willst, ich soll kecklich mich und dich entzünden,
Reichst lächelnd mir den Tod im Kelch der Sünden!

II

Aufgeschmückt ist der Freudensaal.
Lichterhell, bunt, in laulicher Sommernacht
Stehet das offene Gartengezelte.
Säulengleich steigen, gepaart,
5 Grün-umranket, eherne Schlangen,

Zwölf, mit verschlungenen Hälsen,
Tragend und stützend das
Leicht gegitterte Dach.
Aber die Braut noch wartet verborgen
10 In dem Kämmerlein ihres Hauses.
Endlich bewegt sich der Zug der Hochzeit,
Fackeln tragend,
Feierlich stumm.
Und in der Mitte,
15 Mich an der rechten Hand,
Schwarz gekleidet, geht einfach die Braut;
Schöngefaltet ein Scharlachtuch
Liegt um den zierlichen Kopf geschlagen.
Lächelnd geht sie dahin; das Mahl schon duftet.

20 Später im Lärmen des Fests
Stahlen wir seitwärts uns beide
Weg, nach den Schatten des Gartens wandelnd,
Wo im Gebüsche die Rosen brannten,
Wo der Mondstrahl um Lilien zuckte,
25 Wo die Weymouthsfichte mit schwarzem Haar
Den Spiegel des Teiches halb verhängt.

Auf seidnem Rasen dort, ach, Herz am Herzen,
Wie verschlangen, erstickten meine Küsse den scheueren Kuß!
Indes der Springquell, unteilnehmend
30 An überschwenglicher Liebe Geflüster,
Sich ewig des eigenen Plätscherns freute;
Uns aber neckten von fern und lockten
Freundliche Stimmen,
Flöten und Saiten umsonst.

35 Ermüdet lag, zu bald für mein Verlangen,
Das leichte, liebe Haupt auf meinem Schoß.
Spielender Weise mein Aug' auf ihres drückend,
Fühlt' ich ein Weilchen die langen Wimpern,
Bis der Schlaf sie stellte,
40 Wie Schmetterlingsgefieder auf und nieder gehn.

Eh' das Frührot schien,
Eh' das Lämpchen erlosch im Brautgemache,
Weckt' ich die Schläferin,
Führte das seltsame Kind in mein Haus ein.

III

Ein Irrsal kam in die Mondscheingärten
Einer einst heiligen Liebe.
Schaudernd entdeckt' ich verjährten Betrug.
Und mit weinendem Blick, doch grausam,
5 Hieß ich das schlanke,
Zauberhafte Mädchen
Ferne gehen von mir.
Ach, ihre hohe Stirn
War gesenkt, denn sie liebte mich;
10 Aber sie zog mit Schweigen
Fort in die graue
Welt hinaus.

Krank seitdem,
Wund ist und wehe mein Herz.
15 Nimmer wird es genesen!

Als ginge, luftgesponnen, ein Zauberfaden
Von ihr zu mir, ein ängstig Band,
So zieht es, zieht mich schmachtend ihr nach!
— Wie? wenn ich eines Tags auf meiner Schwelle
20 Sie sitzen fände, wie einst, im Morgen-Zwielicht,
Das Wanderbündel neben ihr,
Und ihr Auge, treuherzig zu mir aufschauend,
Sagte, da bin ich wieder
Hergekommen aus weiter Welt!

IV

Warum, Geliebte, denk' ich dein
Auf einmal nun mit tausend Tränen,
Und kann gar nicht zufrieden sein,
Und will die Brust in alle Weite dehnen?

5 Ach, gestern in den hellen Kindersaal,
Beim Flimmer zierlich aufgesteckter Kerzen,
Wo ich mein selbst vergaß in Lärm und Scherzen,
Tratst du, o Bildnis mitleid-schöner Qual;
Es war dein Geist, er setzte sich ans Mahl,
10 Fremd saßen wir mit stumm verhalt'nen Schmerzen;
Zuletzt brach ich in lautes Schluchzen aus,
Und Hand in Hand verließen wir das Haus.

V

Die Liebe, sagt man, steht am Pfahl gebunden,
Geht endlich arm, zerrüttet, unbeschuht;
Dies edle Haupt hat nicht mehr, wo es ruht,
Mit Tränen netzet sie der Füße Wunden.

5 Ach, Peregrinen hab' ich so gefunden!
Schön war ihr Wahnsinn, ihrer Wange Glut,
Noch scherzend in der Frühlingsstürme Wut
Und wilde Kränze in das Haar gewunden.

War's möglich, solche Schönheit zu verlassen?
10 — So kehrt nur reizender das alte Glück!
O komm, in diese Arme dich zu fassen!

Doch weh! o weh! was soll mir dieser Blick?
Sie küßt mich zwischen Lieben noch und Hassen,
Sie kehrt sich ab und kehrt mir nie zurück.

3. AN EINEM WINTERMORGEN, VOR SONNEN-
AUFGANG

O flaumenleichte Zeit der dunkeln Frühe!
Welch neue Welt bewegest du in mir?
Was ist's, daß ich auf einmal nun in dir
Von sanfter Wollust meines Daseins glühe?

5 Einem Krystall gleicht meine Seele nun,
Den noch kein falscher Strahl des Lichts getroffen;
Zu fluten scheint mein Geist, er scheint zu ruhn,
Dem Eindruck naher Wunderkräfte offen,
Die aus dem klaren Gürtel blauer Luft
10 Zuletzt ein Zauberwort vor meine Sinne ruft.

Bei hellen Augen glaub' ich doch zu schwanken;
Ich schließe sie, daß nicht der Traum entweiche.
Seh ich hinab in lichte Feenreiche?
Wer hat den bunten Schwarm von Bildern und Gedanken
15 Zur Pforte meines Herzens hergeladen,
Die glänzend sich in diesem Busen baden,
Goldfarb'gen Fischlein gleich im Gartenteiche?

Ich höre bald der Hirtenflöten Klänge,
Wie um die Krippe jener Wundernacht,
20 Bald weinbekränzter Jugend Lustgesänge;
Wer hat das friedenselige Gedränge
In meine traurigen Wände hergebracht?

Und welch Gefühl entzückter Stärke,
Indem mein Sinn sich frisch zur Ferne lenkt!
25 Vom ersten Mark des heut'gen Tags getränkt,
Fühl' ich mir Mut zu jedem frommen Werke.
Die Seele fliegt, soweit der Himmel reicht,
Der Genius jauchzt in mir! Doch sage,
Warum wird jetzt der Blick von Wehmut feucht?
30 Ist's ein verloren Glück, was mich erweicht?
Ist es ein werdendes, was ich im Herzen trage?
— Hinweg, mein Geist! hier gilt kein Stillestehn:
Es ist ein Augenblick, und alles wird verwehn!

Dort, sieh! am Horizont lüpft sich der Vorhang schon!
35 Es träumt der Tag, nun sei die Nacht entflohn;
Die Purpurlippe, die geschlossen lag,
Haucht, halb geöffnet, süße Atemzüge:
Auf einmal blitzt das Aug', und, wie ein Gott, der Tag
Beginnt im Sprung die königlichen Flüge!

4. GESANG ZU ZWEIEN IN DER NACHT

Sie

Wie süß der Nachtwind nun die Wiese streift
Und klingend jetzt den jungen Hain durchläuft!
Da noch der freche Tag verstummt,
Hört man der Erdenkräfte flüsterndes Gedränge,
5 Das aufwärts in die zärtlichen Gesänge
Der reingestimmten Lüfte summt.

Er

Vernehm' ich doch die wunderbarsten Stimmen,
Vom lauen Wind wollüstig hingeschleift,
Indes, mit ungewissem Licht gestreift,
10 Der Himmel selber scheinet hinzuschwimmen.

Sie

Wie ein Gewebe zuckt die Luft manchmal,
Durchsichtiger und heller aufzuwehen;
Dazwischen hört man weiche Töne gehen
Von sel'gen Feen, die im blauen Saal
15 Zum Sphärenklang,
Und fleißig mit Gesang,
Silberne Spindeln hin und wieder drehen.

Er

O holde Nacht, du gehst mit leisem Tritt
Auf schwarzem Samt, der nur am Tage grünet,
20 Und luftig schwirrender Musik bedienet
Sich nun dein Fuß zum leichten Schritt,
Womit du Stund' um Stunde missest,
Dich lieblich in dir selbst vergissest —
Du schwärmst, es schwärmt der Schöpfung Seele mit!

5. NACHTS

Horch! auf der Erde feuchtem Grund gelegen,
Arbeitet schwer die Nacht der Dämmerung entgegen,
Indessen dort, in blauer Luft gezogen,
Die Fäden leicht, unhörbar fließen
5 Und hin und wieder mit gestähltem Bogen
Die lust'gen Sterne goldne Pfeile schießen.

Im Erdenschoß, im Hain und auf der Flur,
Wie wühlt es jetzo rings in der Natur
Von nimmersatter Kräfte Gärung!
10 Und welche Ruhe doch und welch ein Wohlbedacht!
Mir aber in geheimer Brust erwacht
Ein peinlich Widerspiel von Fülle und Entbehrung
Vor diesem Bild, so schweigend und so groß.
Mein Herz, wie gerne machtest du dich los!
15 Du schwankendes, dem jeder Halt gebricht,
Willst, kaum entflohn, zurück zu deinesgleichen.
Trägst du der Schönheit Götterstille nicht,
So beuge dich! denn hier ist kein Entweichen.

6. JUNG VOLKER

Gesang der Räuber

Jung Volker, das ist unser Räuberhauptmann,
Mit Fiedel und mit Flinte,
Damit er geigen und schießen kann,
Nach dem just Wetter und Winde.
5   Fiedel und die Flint',
           Fiedel und die Flint'!
           Volker spielt auf.

Ich sah ihn hoch im Sonnenschein
Auf einem Hügel sitzen:
10 Da spielt er die Geig' und schluckt roten Wein,
Seine blauen Augen ihm blitzen.
           Fiedel und die Flint',
           Fiedel und die Flint'!
           Volker spielt auf.

15 Auf einmal, er schleudert die Geig' in die Luft,
Auf einmal, er wirft sich zu Pferde:
Der Feind kommt! Da stößt er ins Pfeifchen und ruft:
„Brecht ein, wie der Wolf in die Herde!"
           Fiedel und die Flint',
20   Fiedel und die Flint'!
           Volker spielt auf.

7. JUNG VOLKERS LIED

Und die mich trug im Mutterleib,
Und die mich schwang im Kissen,
Die war ein schön frech braunes Weib,
Wollte nichts vom Mannsvolk wissen.

5 Sie scherzte nur und lachte laut
Und ließ die Freier stehen:
„Möcht' lieber sein des Windes Braut,
Denn in die Ehe gehen!"

Da kam der Wind, da nahm der Wind
10 Als Buhle sie gefangen:
Von dem hat sie ein lustig Kind
In ihren Schoß empfangen.

8. BESUCH IN URACH

Nur fast so wie im Traum ist mir's geschehen,
Daß ich in dies geliebte Tal verirrt.
Kein Wunder ist, was meine Augen sehen,
Doch schwankt der Boden, Luft und Staude schwirrt,
5 Aus tausend grünen Spiegeln scheint zu gehen
Vergangne Zeit, die lächelnd mich verwirrt;
Die Wahrheit selber wird hier zum Gedichte,
Mein eigen Bild ein fremd und hold Gesichte.

Da seid ihr alle wieder aufgerichtet,
10 Besonnte Felsen, alte Wolkenstühle!
Auf Wäldern schwer, wo kaum der Mittag lichtet
Und Schatten mischt mit balsamreicher Schwüle.
Kennt ihr mich noch, der sonst hieher geflüchtet,
Im Moose, bei süßschläferndem Gefühle,
15 Der Mücke Sumsen hier ein Ohr geliehen,
Ach, kennt ihr mich und wollt nicht vor mir fliehen?

Hier wird ein Strauch, ein jeder Halm zur Schlinge,
Die mich in liebliche Betrachtung fängt;
Kein Mäuerchen, kein Holz ist so geringe,
20 Daß nicht mein Blick voll Wehmut an ihm hängt:
Ein jedes spricht mir halbvergeßne Dinge;
Ich fühle, wie von Schmerz und Lust gedrängt
Die Träne stockt, indes ich ohne Weile,
Unschlüssig, satt und durstig, weiter eile.

25 Hinweg! und leite mich, du Schar von Quellen,
Die ihr durchspielt der Matten grünes Gold!
Zeigt mir die urbemoosten Wasserzellen,
Aus denen euer ewig's Leben rollt,
Im kühnsten Walde die verwachsnen Schwellen,
30 Wo eurer Mutter Kraft im Berge grollt,
Bis sie im breiten Schwung an Felsenwänden
Herabstürzt, euch im Tale zu versenden!

Oh, hier ist's, wo Natur den Schleier reißt!
Sie bricht einmal ihr übermenschlich Schweigen;
35 Laut mit sich selber redend, will ihr Geist,
Sich selbst vernehmend, sich ihm selber zeigen. —

— Doch ach, sie bleibt, mehr als der Mensch, verwaist,
Darf nicht aus ihrem eignen Rätsel steigen!
Dir biet' ich denn, begier'ge Wassersäule,
40 Die nackte Brust, ach, ob sie dir sich teile!

Vergebens! und dein kühles Element
Tropft an mir ab, im Grase zu versinken.
Was ist's, das deine Seele von mir trennt?
Sie flieht, und möcht' ich auch in dir ertrinken!
45 Dich kränkt's nicht, wie mein Herz um dich entbrennt,
Küssest im Sturz nur diese schroffen Zinken;
Du bleibest, was du warst seit Tag und Jahren,
Ohn' ein'gen Schmerz der Zeiten zu erfahren.

Hinweg aus diesem üpp'gen Schattengrund
50 Voll großer Pracht, die drückend mich erschüttert!
Bald grüßt beruhigt mein verstummter Mund
Den schlichten Winkel, wo sonst halb verwittert
Die kleine Bank und wo das Hüttchen stund;
Erinnrung reicht mit Lächeln die verbittert
55 Bis zur Betäubung süßen Zauberschalen!
So trink ich gierig die entzückten Qualen.

Hier schlang sich tausendmal ein junger Arm
Um meinen Hals mit inn'gem Wohlgefallen.
O säh' ich mich, als Knaben sonder Harm,
60 Wie einst, mit Necken durch die Haine wallen!
Ihr Hügel, von der *alten* Sonne warm,
Erscheint mir denn auf keinem von euch allen
Mein Ebenbild, in jugendlicher Frische
Hervorgesprungen aus dem Waldgebüsche?

65 O komm, enthülle dich! dann sollst du mir
Mit Freundlichkeit ins dunkle Auge schauen!
Noch immer, guter Knabe, gleich' ich dir,
Uns beiden wird nicht voreinander grauen.
So komm und laß mich unaufhaltsam hier
70 Mich deinem reinen Busen anvertrauen! —
Umsonst, daß ich die Arme nach dir strecke,
Den Boden, wo du gingst, mit Küssen decke!

Hier will ich denn laut schluchzend liegen bleiben,
Fühllos, und alles habe seinen Lauf!

75 Mein Finger, matt, ins Gras beginnt zu schreiben:
„Hin ist die Lust! hab' alles seinen Lauf!"
Da plötzlich hör' ich's durch die Lüfte treiben,
Und ein entfernter Donner schreckt mich auf;
Elastisch angespannt mein ganzes Wesen
80 Ist von Gewitterluft wie neu genesen.

Sieh, wie die Wolken finstre Ballen schließen
Um den ehrwürd'gen Trotz der Burgruine!
Von weitem schon hört man den alten Riesen,
Stumm harrt das Tal mit ungewisser Miene,
85 Der Kuckuck nur ruft sein einförmig Grüßen
Versteckt aus unerforschter Wildnis Grüne, —
Jetzt kracht die Wölbung und verhallet lange,
Das wundervolle Schauspiel ist im Gange!

Ja nun, indes mit hoher Feuerhelle
90 Der Blitz die Stirn und Wange mir verklärt,
Ruf' ich den lauten Segen in die grelle
Musik des Donners, die mein Wort bewährt:
O Tal! du meines Lebens andre Schwelle!
Du meiner tiefsten Kräfte stiller Herd!
95 Du meiner Liebe Wundernest! ich scheide,
Leb' wohl! — und sei dein Engel mein Geleite!

9. SEPTEMBERMORGEN

Im Nebel ruhet noch die Welt,
Noch träumen Wald und Wiesen:
Bald siehst du, wenn der Schleier fällt,
Den blauen Himmel unverstellt,
5 Herbstkräftig die gedämpfte Welt
In warmem Golde fließen.

10. UM MITTERNACHT

Gelassen stieg die Nacht ans Land,
Lehnt träumend an der Berge Wand,
Ihr Auge sieht die goldne Wage nun
Der Zeit in gleichen Schalen stille ruhn;
5 Und kecker rauschen die Quellen hervor,

      Sie singen der Mutter, der Nacht, ins Ohr
        Vom Tage,
    Vom heute gewesenen Tage.

      Das uralt alte Schlummerlied,
10 Sie achtet's nicht, sie ist es müd';
      Ihr klingt des Himmels Bläue süßer noch,
      Der flücht'gen Stunden gleichgeschwungnes Joch.
        Doch immer behalten die Quellen das Wort,
        Es singen die Wasser im Schlafe noch fort
15   Vom Tage.
    Vom heute gewesenen Tage.

11. IM FRÜHLING

    Hier lieg' ich auf dem Frühlingshügel:
    Die Wolke wird mein Flügel,
    Ein Vogel fliegt mir voraus.
    Ach, sag' mir, alleinzige Liebe,
5 Wo du bleibst, daß ich bei dir bliebe!
    Doch du und die Lüfte, ihr habt kein Haus.

    Der Sonnenblume gleich steht mein Gemüte offen,
    Sehnend,
    Sich dehnend
10 In Lieben und Hoffen.
    Frühling, was bist du gewillt?
    Wann werd' ich gestillt?

    Die Wolke seh' ich wandeln und den Fluß,
    Es dringt der Sonne goldner Kuß
15 Mir tief bis ins Geblüt hinein;
    Die Augen, wunderbar berauschet,
    Tun, als schliefen sie ein,
    Nur noch das Ohr dem Ton der Biene lauschet.
    Ich denke dies und denke das,
20 Ich sehne mich, und weiß nicht recht nach was:
    Halb ist es Lust, halb ist es Klage;
    Mein Herz, o sage,
    Was webst du für Erinnerung
    In golden grüner Zweige Dämmerung?
25 —Alte unnennbare Tage!

12. FRAGE UND ANTWORT

Fragst du mich, woher die bange
Liebe mir zum Herzen kam,
Und warum ich ihr nicht lange
Schon den bittern Stachel nahm?

5 Sprich warum mit Geisterschnelle
Wohl der Wind die Flügel rührt,
Und woher die süße Quelle
Die verborgnen Wasser führt?

Banne du auf seiner Fährte
10 Mir den Wind in vollem Lauf!
Halte mit der Zaubergerte
Du die süßen Quellen auf!

13. NIMMERSATTE LIEBE

So ist die Lieb'! So ist die Lieb'!
Mit Küssen nicht zu stillen:
Wer ist der Tor und will ein Sieb
Mit eitel Wasser füllen?
5 Und schöpfst du an die tausend Jahr'
Und küssest ewig, ewig gar,
Du tust ihr nie zu Willen.

Die Lieb', die Lieb' hat alle Stund'
Neu wunderlich Gelüsten;
10 Wir bissen uns die Lippen wund,
Da wir uns heute küßten.
Das Mädchen hielt in guter Ruh',
Wie's Lämmlein unterm Messer;
Ihr Auge bat: „Nur immer zu!
15 Je weher, desto besser!"

So ist die Lieb'! und war auch so,
Wie lang' es Liebe gibt,
Und anders war Herr Salomo,
Der Weise, nicht verliebt.

14. AUF DER REISE

Zwischen süßem Schmerz,
Zwischen dumpfem Wohlbehagen
Sitz’ ich nächtlich in dem Reisewagen,
Lasse mich so weit von dir, mein Herz,
5 Weit und immer weiter tragen.

Schweigend sitz’ ich und allein,
Ich wiege mich in bunten Träumen,
Das muntre Posthorn klingt darein,
Es tanzt der liebe Mondenschein
10 Nach diesem Ton auf Quellen und auf Bäumen,
Sogar zu mir durchs enge Fensterlein.

Ich wünsche mir nun dies und das.
O könnt’ ich jetzo durch ein Zauberglas
Ins Goldgewebe deines Traumes blicken!
15 Vielleicht dann säh’ ich wieder mit Entzücken
Dich in der Laube wohlbekannt.
Ich sähe Genovevens Hand
Auf deiner Schulter traulich liegen,
Am Ende säh’ ich selber mich,
20 Halb keck und halb bescheidentlich,
An deine holde Wange schmiegen.

Doch nein! wie dürft’ ich auch nur hoffen,
Daß jetzt mein Schatten bei dir sei!
Ach, stünden deine Träume für mich offen,
25 Du winktest wohl auch wachend mich herbei!

15. LIED VOM WINDE

Sausewind, Brausewind,
Dort und hier!
Deine Heimat sage mir!

„Kindlein, wir fahren
5 Seit viel vielen Jahren
Durch die weit weite Welt,
Und möchten’s erfragen,

Die Antwort erjagen
Bei den Bergen, den Meeren,
10 Bei des Himmels klingenden Heeren:
Die wissen es nie.
Bist du klüger als sie,
Magst du es sagen.
— Fort, wohlauf!
15 Halt uns nicht auf!
Kommen andre nach, unsre Brüder,
Da frag wieder!"

Halt an! Gemach,
Eine kleine Frist!
20 Sagt, wo der Liebe Heimat ist,
Ihr Anfang, ihr Ende?

„Wer's nennen könnte!
Schelmisches Kind,
Lieb' ist wie Wind,
25 Rasch und lebendig,
Ruhet nie,
Ewig ist sie,
Aber nicht immer beständig.
— Fort! Wohlauf! auf!
30 Halt uns nicht auf!
Fort über Stoppel und Wälder und Wiesen!
Wenn ich dein Schätzchen seh',
Will ich es grüßen.
Kindlein, ade!"

16. ANTIKE POESIE

Ich sah den Helikon in Wolkendunst,
Nur kaum berührt vom ersten Sonnenstrahle:
Schau! jetzo stehen hoch mit *einem* Male
Die Gipfel dort in Morgenrötebrunst.

5 Hier unten spricht von keuscher Musen Gunst
Der heil'ge Quell im dunkelgrünen Tale;
Wer aber schöpft mit reiner Opferschale,
Wie einst, den echten Tau der alten Kunst?

Wie? soll ich endlich keinen Meister sehn?
10 Will keiner mehr den alten Lorbeer pflücken?
— Da sah ich Iphigeniens Dichter stehn:

Er ist's, an dessen Blick sich diese Höhn
So zauberhaft, so sonnewarm erquicken.
Er geht, und frostig rauhe Lüfte wehn.

17. MEIN FLUSZ

O Fluß, mein Fluß im Morgenstrahl!
Empfange nun, empfange
Den sehnsuchtsvollen Leib einmal
Und küsse Brust und Wange!
5 — Er fühlt mir schon herauf die Brust,
Er kühlt mit Liebesschauerlust
Und jauchzendem Gesange.

Es schlüpft der goldne Sonnenschein
In Tropfen an mir nieder,
10 Die Woge wieget aus und ein
Die hingegebnen Glieder;
Die Arme hab' ich ausgespannt,
Sie kommt auf mich herzugerannt,
Sie faßt und läßt mich wieder.

15 Du murmelst so, mein Fluß, warum?
Du trägst seit alten Tagen
Ein seltsam Märchen mit dir um
Und mühst dich, es zu sagen;
Du eilst so sehr und läufst so sehr,
20 Als müßtest du im Land umher,
Man weiß nicht wen, drum fragen.

Der Himmel, blau und kinderrein,
Worin die Wellen singen,
Der Himmel ist die Seele dein:
25 O laß mich ihn durchdringen!
Ich tauche mich mit Geist und Sinn
Durch die vertiefte Bläue hin
Und kann sie nicht erschwingen!

Was ist so tief, so tief wie sie?
30 Die Liebe nur alleine.
Sie wird nicht satt und sättigt nie
Mit ihrem Wechselscheine.
— Schwill an, mein Fluß, und hebe dich!
Mit Grausen übergieße mich!
35 Mein Leben um das deine!

Du weisest schmeichelnd mich zurück
Zu deiner Blumenschwelle.
So trage denn allein dein Glück
Und wieg auf deiner Welle
40 Der Sonne Pracht, des Mondes Ruh':
Nach tausend Irren kehrest du
Zur ew'gen Mutterquelle!

18. DIE TRAURIGE KRÖNUNG

Es war ein König Milesint,
Von dem will ich euch sagen:
Der meuchelte sein Bruderskind,
Wollte selbst die Krone tragen.
5 Die Krönung ward mit Prangen
Auf Liffey-Schloß begangen.
O Irland! Irland! warest du so blind?

Der König sitzt um Mitternacht
Im leeren Marmorsaale,
10 Sieht irr' in all die neue Pracht,
Wie trunken von dem Mahle;
Er spricht zu seinem Sohne:
,,Noch einmal bring' die Krone!
Doch schau, wer hat die Pforten aufgemacht?"

15 Da kommt ein seltsam Totenspiel,
Ein Zug mit leisen Tritten,
Vermummte Gäste groß und viel,
Eine Krone schwankt inmitten;
Es drängt sich durch die Pforte
20 Mit Flüstern ohne Worte;
Dem Könige, dem wird so geisterschwül.

Und aus der schwarzen Menge blickt
Ein Kind mit frischer Wunde,
Es lächelt sterbensweh und nickt,
25 Es macht im Saal die Runde,
Es trippelt zu dem Throne,
Es reichet eine Krone
Dem Könige, des Herze tief erschrickt.

Darauf der Zug von dannen strich,
30 Von Morgenluft berauschet,
Die Kerzen flackern wunderlich,
Der Mond am Fenster lauschet;
Der Sohn mit Angst und Schweigen
Zum Vater tät sich neigen, —
35 Er neiget über eine Leiche sich.

19. IN DER FRÜHE

Kein Schlaf noch kühlt das Auge mir,
Dort gehet schon der Tag herfür
An meinem Kammerfenster.
Es wühlet mein verstörter Sinn
5 Noch zwischen Zweifeln her und hin
Und schaffet Nachtgespenster.
Ängste, quäle
Dich nicht länger, meine Seele!
Freu' dich! schon sind da und dorten
10 Morgenglocken wach geworden.

20. DIE GEISTER AM MUMMELSEE

Vom Berge was kommt dort um Mitternacht spät
Mit Fackeln so prächtig herunter?
Ob das wohl zum Tanze, zum Feste noch geht?
Mir klingen die Lieder so munter.
5   O nein!
So sage, was mag es wohl sein?

Das, was du da siehest, ist Totengeleit,
Und was du da hörest, sind Klagen.
Dem König, dem Zauberer, gilt es zu Leid,

10 Sie bringen ihn wieder getragen.
                        O weh!
   So sind es die Geister vom See!

   Sie schweben herunter ins Mummelseetal —
   Sie haben den See schon betreten —
15 Sie rühren und netzen den Fuß nicht einmal —
   Sie schwirren in leisen Gebeten —
                        O schau,
   Am Sarge die glänzende Frau!

   Jetzt öffnet der See das grünspiegelnde Tor;
20 Gib acht, nun tauchen sie nieder!
   Es schwankt eine lebende Treppe hervor,
   Und — drunten schon summen die Lieder.
                        Hörst du?
   Sie singen ihn unten zur Ruh'.

25 Die Wasser, wie lieblich sie brennen und glühn!
   Sie spielen in grünendem Feuer;
   Es geisten die Nebel am Ufer dahin,
   Zum Meere verzieht sich der Weiher —
                        Nur still!
30 Ob dort sich nichts rührn will?

   Es zuckt in der Mitten — o Himml! ach hilf!
   Nun kommen sie wieder, sie kommen!
   Es orgelt im Rohr, und es klirret im Schilf;
   Nur hurtig, die Flucht nur gnommn!
35   Davon!
   Sie wittern, sie haschen mich schon!

21. ER IST'S

   Frühling läßt sein blaues Band
   Wieder flattern durch die Lüfte;
   Süße, wohlbekannte Düfte
   Streifen ahnungsvoll das Land.
5 Veilchen träumen schon,
   Wollen balde kommen.
   — Horch, von fern ein leiser Harfenton!
   Frühling, ja du bist's!
   Dich hab' ich vernommen!

22. DAS VERLASSENE MÄGDLEIN

Früh, wann die Hähne krähn,
Eh' die Sternlein verschwinden,
Muß ich am Herde stehn,
Muß Feuer zünden.

5 Schön ist der Flammen Schein,
Es springen die Funken;
Ich schaue so drein,
In Leid versunken.

Plötzlich, da kommt es mir,
10 Treuloser Knabe,
Daß ich die Nacht von dir
Geträumet habe.

Träne auf Träne dann
Stürzet hernieder;
15 So kommt der Tag heran —
O ging' er wieder!

23. BEGEGNUNG

Was doch heut' nacht ein Sturm gewesen,
Bis erst der Morgen sich geregt!
Wie hat der ungebetne Besen
Kamin und Gassen ausgefegt!

5 Da kommt ein Mädchen schon die Straßen,
Das halb verschüchtert um sich sieht;
Wie Rosen, die der Wind zerblasen,
So unstet ihr Gesichtchen glüht.

Ein schöner Bursch tritt ihr entgegen,
10 Er will ihr voll Entzücken nahn;
Wie sehn sich freudig und verlegen
Die ungewohnten Schelme an!

Er scheint zu fragen, ob das Liebchen
Die Zöpfe schon zurecht gemacht,
15 Die heute nacht im offnen Stübchen
Ein Sturm in Unordnung gebracht.

Der Bursche träumt noch von den Küssen,
Die ihm das süße Kind getauscht,
Er steht, von Anmut hingerissen,
20 Derweil sie um die Ecke rauscht.

24. SEHNSUCHT

In dieser Winterfrühe
Wie ist mir doch zumut!
O Morgenrot, ich glühe
Von deinem Jugendblut.

5 Es glüht der alte Felsen
Und Wald und Burg zumal,
Berauschte Nebel wälzen
Sich jäh hinab das Tal.

Mit tatenfroher Eile
10 Erhebt sich Geist und Sinn,
Und flügelt goldne Pfeile
Durch alle Ferne hin.

Auf Zinnen möcht' ich springen
In alter Fürsten Schloß
15 Möcht' hohe Lieder singen,
Mich schwingen auf das Roß!

Und stolzen Siegeswagen
Stürzt' ich mich brausend nach!
Die Harfe wird zerschlagen,
20 Die nur von Liebe sprach.

— Wie? schwärmst du so vermessen,
Herz, hast du nicht bedacht,
Hast du mit eins vergessen,
Was dich so trunken macht?

25 Ach wohl! was aus mir singet,
Ist nur der Liebe Glück,
Die wirren Töne schlinget
Sie sanft in sich zurück.

Was hilft, was hilft mein Sehnen?
30 Geliebte, wärst du hier!
In tausend Freudetränen
Verging' die Erde mir.

25. KARWOCHE

O Woche, Zeugin heiliger Beschwerde!
Du stimmst so ernst zu dieser Frühlingswonne,
Du breitest im verjüngten Strahl der Sonne
Des Kreuzes Schatten auf die lichte Erde,

5 Und senkest schweigend deine Flöre nieder;
Der Frühling darf indessen immer keimen,
Das Veilchen duftet unter Blütenbäumen,
Und alle Vöglein singen Jubellieder.

O schweigt, ihr Vöglein auf den grünen Auen!
10 Es hallen rings die dumpfen Glockenklänge,
Die Engel singen leise Grabgesänge;
O still, ihr Vöglein hoch im Himmelblauen!

Ihr Veilchen, kränzt heut keine Lockenhaare!
Euch pflückt mein frommes Kind zum dunkeln Strauße,
15 Ihr wandert mit zum Muttergotteshause,
Da sollt ihr welken auf des Herrn Altare.

Ach dort, von Trauermelodien trunken
Und süß betäubt von schweren Weihrauchdüften,
Sucht sie den Bräutigam in Todesgrüften
20 Und Lieb' und Frühling, alles ist versunken.

26. ZU VIEL

Der Himmel glänzt vom reinsten Frühlingslichte,
Ihm schwillt der Hügel sehnsuchtsvoll entgegen,
Die starre Welt zerfließt in Liebessegen
Und schmiegt sich rund zum zärtlichsten Gedichte.

5 Am Dorfeshang, dort bei der luft'gen Fichte,
Ist meiner Liebsten kleines Haus gelegen —
O Herz, was hilft dein Wiegen und dein Wägen,
Daß all der Wonnestreit in dir sich schlichte!

Du, Liebe, hilf den süßen Zauber lösen,
10 Womit Natur in meinem Innern wühlet!
Und du, o Frühling, hilf die Liebe beugen!

Lisch aus, o Tag! Laß mich in Nacht genesen!
Indes ihr sanften Sterne göttlich kühlet,
Will ich zum Abgrund der Betrachtung steigen.

27. ELFENLIED

Bei Nacht im Dorf der Wächter rief:
        Elfe!
Ein ganz kleines Elfchen im Walde schlief —
        Wohl um die Elfe! —
5 Und meint, es rief ihm aus dem Tal
Bei seinem Namen die Nachtigall,
Oder Silpelit hätt' ihm gerufen.
Reibt sich der Elf die Augen aus,
Begibt sich vor sein Schneckenhaus
10 Und ist als wie ein trunken Mann,
Sein Schläflein war nicht voll getan,
Und humpelt also tippe tapp
Durchs Haselholz ins Tal hinab,
Schlupft an der Mauer hin so dicht,
15 Da sitzt der Glühwurm, Licht an Licht.
Was sind das helle Fensterlein?
Da drin wird eine Hochzeit sein:
Die Kleinen sitzen beim Mahle
Und treiben's in dem Saale;
20 Da guck' ich wohl ein wenig 'nein!
— Pfui, stößt den Kopf an harten Stein!
Elfe, gelt, du hast genug?
        Guckuck! Guckuck!

28. AGNES

Rosenzeit! wie schnell vorbei,
        Schnell vorbei
Bist du doch gegangen!
Wär' mein Lieb nur blieben treu,
5   Blieben treu,
Sollte mir nicht bangen.

Um die Ernte wohlgemut,
    Wohlgemut
Schnitterinnen singen.
10 Aber ach! mir kranken Blut,
    Mir kranken Blut
Will nichts mehr gelingen.

Schleiche so durchs Wiesental,
    So durchs Tal,
15 Als im Traum verloren,
Nach dem Berg, da tausendmal
    Tausendmal
Er mir Treu' geschworen.

Oben auf des Hügels Rand,
20   Abgewandt,
Wein' ich bei der Linde;
An dem Hut mein Rosenband,
    Von seiner Hand,
Spielet in dem Winde.

29. VERBORGENHEIT

Laß, o Welt, o laß mich sein!
Locket nicht mit Liebesgaben,
Laßt dies Herz alleine haben
Seine Wonne, seine Pein!

5 Was ich traure, weiß ich nicht,
Es ist unbekanntes Wehe;
Immerdar durch Tränen sehe
Ich der Sonne liebes Licht.

Oft bin ich mir kaum bewußt,
10 Und die helle Freude zücket
Durch die Schwere, so mich drücket,
Wonniglich in meiner Brust.

Laß, o Welt, o laß mich sein!
Locket nicht mit Liebesgaben,
15 Laßt dies Herz alleine haben
Seine Wonne, seine Pein!

30. SEUFZER

(Altes Lied)

Jesu benigne!
A cujus igne
Opto flagrare
Et Te amare:
Cur non flagravi?
Cur non amavi
Te, Jesu Christe?
— O frigus triste!

Dein Liebesfeuer,
Ach, Herr! wie teuer
Wollt' ich es hegen,
Wollt' ich es pflegen!
5 Hab's nicht geheget,
Und nicht gepfleget,
Bin tot im Herzen —
O Höllenschmerzen!

31. GEBET

Herr! schicke, was du willt,
Ein Liebes oder Leides;
Ich bin vergnügt, daß beides
Aus deinen Händen quillt.

5 Wollest mit Freuden
Und wollest mit Leiden
Mich nicht überschütten!
Doch in der Mitten
Liegt holdes Bescheiden.

32. ZUM NEUEN JAHR

Kirchengesang

Wie heimlicher Weise
Ein Engelein leise
Mit rosigen Füßen
Die Erde betritt,

5 So nahte der Morgen.
Jauchzt ihm, ihr Frommen,
Ein heilig Willkommen,
Ein heilig Willkommen!
Herz, jauchze du mit!

10 In Ihm sei's begonnen,
Der Monde und Sonnen
An blauen Gezelten
Des Himmels bewegt.
Du, Vater, du rate!
15 Lenke du und wende!
Herr, dir in die Hände
Sei Anfang und Ende,
Sei alles gelegt!

33. ABSCHIED

Unangeklopft ein Herr tritt abends bei mir ein:
„Ich habe die Ehr', Ihr Rezensent zu sein."
Sofort nimmt er das Licht in die Hand,
Besieht lang meinen Schatten an der Wand,
5 Rückt nah und fern: „Nun, lieber junger Mann,
Sehn Sie doch gefälligst mal Ihre Nas' so von der Seite an!
Sie geben zu, daß das ein Auswuchs is." —
— Das? Alle Wetter — gewiß —
Ei Hasen! ich dachte nicht,
10 All mein Lebtage nicht,
Daß ich so eine Weltsnase führt' im Gesicht!!

Der Mann sprach noch verschiednes hin und her,
Ich weiß, auf meine Ehre, nicht mehr;
Meinte vielleicht, ich sollt' ihm beichten.
15 Zuletzt stand er auf; ich tat ihm leuchten.
Wie wir nun an der Treppe sind,
Da geb' ich ihm, ganz froh gesinnt,
Einen kleinen Tritt
Nur so von hinten aufs Gesäße mit —
20 Alle Hagel! ward das ein Gerumpel,
Ein Gepurzel, ein Gehumpel!
Dergleichen hab' ich nie gesehn,
All mein Lebtage nicht gesehn,
Einen Menschen so rasch die Trepp' hinabgehn!

34. AN MEINEN VETTER
Juni 1837

Lieber Vetter! Er ist eine
Von den freundlichen Naturen,
Die ich *Sommerwesten* nenne.
Denn sie haben wirklich etwas
5 Sonniges in ihrem Wesen.
Es sind weltliche Beamte,
Rechnungsräte, Revisoren
Oder Kameralverwalter,
Auch wohl manchmal Herrn vom Handel,
10 Aber meist vom ältern Schlage,
Keineswegs *Petit-maîtres*,
Haben manchmal hübsche Bäuche,
Und ihr Vaterland ist Schwaben.

Neulich auf der Reise traf ich
15 Auch mit einer Sommerweste
In der Post zu Besigheim
Eben zu Mittag zusammen.
Und wir speisten eine Suppe,
Darin rote Krebse schwammen,
20 Rindfleisch mit französ'schem Senfe,
Dazu liebliche Radieschen,
Dann Gemüse und so weiter;
Schwatzten von der neusten Zeitung,
Und daß es an manchen Orten
25 Gestern stark gewittert habe.
Drüber zieht der wackre Herr ein
Silbern Büchslein aus der Tasche,
Sich die Zähne auszustochern;
Endlich stopft er sich zum schwarzen
30 Kaffee seine Meerschaumpfeife,
Dampft und diskuriert und schaut in-
mittelst einmal nach den Pferden.

Und ich sah ihm so von hinten
Nach und dachte: Ach, wie diese
35 Lieben, hellen Sommerwesten,
Die bequemen, angenehmen,
Endlich doch auch sterben müssen!

35. AN DENSELBEN

als er sich leidenschaftlich mit Verfertigung von Sonnenuhren
beschäftigte. Mai 1840.

Hör' Er nur einmal, Herr Vetter,
Was mir diese Nacht geträumet!
Sonntag war es, nach Mittage,
Und ich sah vom Fenster Seines
5 Alten gelben Gartenhäuschens,
Wie die Bürgersleute ruhig
Vor der Stadt spazieren gingen.
Und ich wandte mich und sah Ihn,
Der im Anfang nicht zugegen,
10 Ernsthaft vor dem Spiegel stehen
In der Stellung eines Mannes,
Der sich zu balbieren trachtet.
Doch indem ich näher trete,
Muß ich voll Erstaunen sehen,
15 Wie er sich mit schwarzer Farbe
Auf Sein rundes Vollmondantlitz
Einen saubern Halbkreis malte;
Von der linken Schläfe abwärts,
Zwischen Mund und Kinn hindurch und
20 So hinauf die rechte Backe.
Jetzo mit geübtem Pinsel
Zeichnet' Er entlang dem Zirkel
Schöngeformte röm'sche Ziffern,
Kunstgerecht, von eins bis zwölfe.
25 Und ich dachte: ach, mein lieber
Vetter ist ein Narr geworden! —
Denn Er sah mich an mit Augen,
Die mich nicht zu kennen schienen.
Überdem stellt' Er sich förmlich
30 An das Fenster in die Sonne,
Und der Schatten Seiner Nase
Sollte nun die Stunde weisen.
Ach, die Leute auf der Straße
Wollten fast sich Kröpfe lachen!

35 Was nun dieser Traum bedeute?
Ich will Ihn just nicht erschrecken:
Aber laß Er Sein verdammtes
Sonnenuhrenmachen bleiben!

36. DER KNABE UND DAS IMMLEIN

Im Weinberg auf der Höhe
Ein Häuslein steht so windebang,
Hat weder Tür noch Fenster,
Die Weile wird ihm lang.

5 Und ist der Tag so schwüle,
Sind all verstummt die Vögelein,
Summt an der Sonnenblume
Ein Immlein ganz allein.

Mein Lieb hat einen Garten,
10 Da steht ein hübsches Immenhaus:
Kommst du daher geflogen?
Schickt sie dich nach mir aus?

„O nein, du feiner Knabe,
Es hieß mich niemand Boten gehn;
15 Dies Kind weiß nichts vom Lieben,
Hat dich noch kaum gesehn.

Was wüßten auch die Mädchen,
Wenn sie kaum aus der Schule sind!
Dein herzallerliebstes Schätzchen
20 Ist noch ein Mutterkind.

Ich bring' ihm Wachs und Honig;
Adel — ich hab' ein ganzes Pfund;
Wie wird das Schätzchen lachen!
Ihm wässert schon der Mund."

25 Ach, wolltest du ihr sagen,
Ich wüßte, was viel süßer ist:
Nichts Lieblichers auf Erden,
Als wenn man herzt und küßt!

37. DER GÄRTNER

Auf ihrem Leibrößlein,
So weiß wie der Schnee,
Die schönste Prinzessin
Reit't durch die Allee.

5 Der Weg, den das Rößlein
Hintanzet so hold,
Der Sand, den ich streute,
Er blinket wie Gold.

Du rosenfarbs Hütlein,
10 Wohl auf und wohl ab,
O wirf eine Feder
Verstohlen herab!

Und willst du dagegen
Eine Blüte von mir,
15 Nimm tausend für *eine*,
Nimm alle dafür!

38. DIE SOLDATENBRAUT

Ach, wenn's nur der König auch wüßt',
Wie wacker mein Schätzelein ist!
Für den König, da ließ' er sein Blut,
Für mich aber ebensogut.

5 Mein Schatz hat kein Band und kein' Stern,
Kein Kreuz wie die vornehmen Herrn,
Mein Schatz wird auch kein General;
Hätt' er nur seinen Abschied einmal!

Es scheinen drei Sterne so hell
10 Dort über Marien-Kapell';
Da knüpft uns ein rosenrot Band,
Und ein Hauskreuz ist auch bei der Hand.

39. DER TAMBOUR

Wenn meine Mutter hexen könnt',
Da müßt' sie mit dem Regiment
Nach Frankreich, überall mit hin,
Und wär' die Marketenderin.
5 Im Lager, wohl um Mitternacht,
Wenn niemand auf ist als die Wacht
Und alles schnarchet, Roß und Mann,
Vor meiner Trommel säß' ich dann:

Die Trommel müßt' eine Schüssel sein,
10 Ein warmes Sauerkraut darein,
Die Schlegel Messer und Gabel,
Eine lange Wurst mein Sabel;
Mein Tschako wär' ein Humpen gut,
Den füll' ich mit Burgunderblut.
15 Und weil es mir an Lichte fehlt,
Da scheint der Mond in mein Gezelt;
Scheint er auch auf Franzö'sch herein,
Mir fällt doch meine Liebste ein:
Ach weh! jetzt hat der Spaß ein End'!
20 — Wenn nur meine Mutter hexen könnt'!

40. AN EINE ÄOLSHARFE

Tu semper urges flebilibus modis
Mysten ademptum: nec tibi Vesper
Surgente decedunt amores,
Nec rapidum fugiente Solem.   *Hor.*

Angelehnt an die Efeuwand
Dieser alten Terrasse,
Du, einer luftgebornen Muse
Geheimnisvolles Saitenspiel,
5 Fang an,
Fange wieder an
Deine melodische Klage!

Ihr kommet, Winde, fern herüber,
Ach! von des Knaben,
10 Der mir so lieb war,
Frisch grünendem Hügel.
Und Frühlingsblüten unterweges streifend,
Übersättigt mit Wohlgerüchen,
Wie süß bedrängt ihr dies Herz!
15 Und säuselt her in die Saiten,
Angezogen von wohllautender Wehmut,
Wachsend im Zug meiner Sehnsucht,
Und hinsterbend wieder.

Aber auf einmal,
20 Wie der Wind heftiger herstößt,
Ein holder Schrei der Harfe

Wiederholt, mir zu süßem Erschrecken,
Meiner Seele plötzliche Regung;
Und hier — die volle Rose streut, geschüttelt,
25 All ihre Blätter vor meine Füße!

41. AN MEINE MUTTER

Siehe! von allen den Liedern nicht *eines* gilt dir, o Mutter!
Dich zu preisen, o glaub's, bin ich zu arm und zu reich.
Ein noch ungesungenes Lied, ruhst du mir im Busen,
Keinem vernehmbar sonst, mich nur zu trösten bestimmt,
5 Wenn sich das Herz unmutig der Welt abwendet und einsam
Seines himmlischen Teils bleibenden Frieden bedenkt.

42. AUF EIN ALTES BILD

In grüner Landschaft Sommerflor,
Bei kühlem Wasser, Schilf und Rohr,
Schau, wie das Knäblein Sündelos
Frei spielet auf der Jungfrau Schoß!
5 Und dort im Walde wonnesam,
Ach, grünet schon des Kreuzes Stamm!

43. TROST

Ja, mein Glück, das lang gewohnte,
Endlich hat es mich verlassen!
— Ja, die liebsten Freunde seh' ich
Achselzuckend von mir weichen,
5 Und die gnadenreichen Götter,
Die am besten Hülfe wüßten,
Kehren höhnisch mir den Rücken.
Was beginnen? werd' ich etwa,
Meinen Lebenstag verwünschend,
10 Rasch nach Gift und Messer greifen?
Das sei ferne! vielmehr muß man
Stille sich im Herzen fassen.

Und ich sprach zu meinem Herzen:
„Laß uns fest zusammenhalten!
15 Denn wir kennen uns einander,

Wie ihr Nest die Schwalbe kennet,
Wie die Zither kennt den Sänger,
Wie sich Schwert und Schild erkennen,
Schild und Schwert einander lieben.
20 Solch ein Paar, wer scheidet es?"

Als ich dieses Wort gesprochen,
Hüpfte mir das Herz im Busen,
Das noch erst geweinet hatte.

44. EIN STÜNDLEIN WOHL VOR TAG

Derweil ich schlafend lag,
Ein Stündlein wohl vor Tag,
Sang vor dem Fenster auf dem Baum
Ein Schwälblein mir, ich hört' es kaum,
5 Ein Stündlein wohl vor Tag:

„Hör an, was ich dir sag'!
Dein Schätzlein ich verklag':
Derweil ich dieses singen tu',
Herzt er ein Lieb in guter Ruh',
10 Ein Stündlein wohl vor Tag."

O weh! nicht weiter sag!
O still! nichts hören mag!
Flieg ab, flieg ab von meinem Baum!
— Ach, Lieb' und Treu' ist wie ein Traum
15 Ein Stündlein wohl vor Tag.

45. JÄGERLIED

Zierlich ist des Vogels Tritt im Schnee,
Wenn er wandelt auf des Berges Höh':
Zierlicher schreibt Liebchens liebe Hand,
Schreibt ein Brieflein mir in ferne Land'.

5 In die Lüfte hoch ein Reiher steigt,
Dahin weder Pfeil noch Kugel fleugt:
Tausendmal so hoch und so geschwind
Die Gedanken treuer Liebe sind.

46. THEOKRIT

Sei, o Theokritos, mir, du Anmutsvollster gepriesen!
  Lieblich bist du zuerst, aber auch herrlich fürwahr.
Wenn du die Chariten schickst in die Goldpaläste der Reichen,
  Unbeschenkt kehren sie dir, nackenden Fußes, zurück.
5 Müßig sitzen sie wieder im ärmlichen Hause des Dichters,
  Auf die frierenden Knie' traurig die Stirne gesenkt.
Oder die Jungfrau führe mir vor, die, rasend in Liebe,
  Da ihr der Jüngling entfloh, Hekates Künste versucht.
Oder besinge den jungen Herakles, welchem zur Wiege
10 Dienet der eherne Schild, wo er die Schlangen erwürgt:
Klangvoll fährst du dahin! dich kränzte Kalliope selber,
  Aber bescheiden, ein Hirt, kehrst du zur Flöte zurück.

47. MÄRCHEN VOM SICHERN MANN

Soll ich vom sicheren Mann ein Märchen erzählen, so höret!
— Etliche sagen, ihn habe die steinerne Kröte geboren.
Also heißet ein mächtiger Fels in den Bergen des Schwarz-
    walds,
Stumpf und breit, voll Warzen, der häßlichen Kröte ver-
    gleichbar.
5 Darin lag er und schlief bis nach den Tagen der Sündflut.
Nämlich es war sein Vater ein Waldmensch, tückisch und
    grausam,
Allen Göttern ein Greu'l und allen Nymphen gefürchtet.
Ihm nicht durchaus gleich ist der Sohn, doch immer ein
    Unhold;
Riesenhaft an Gestalt, von breitem Rücken und Schultern.
10 Eh'mals ging er fast nackt, unehrbarlich; aber seit Men-
    schen-
  Denken im rauh grauhärenen Rock, mit schrecklichen
    Stiefeln.
Grauliche Borsten bedecken sein Haupt, und es starret der
    Bart ihm.
(Heimlich besucht ihn, heißt es, der Igelslocher Balbierer
In der Höhle, woselbst er ihm dient wie der sorgsame
    Gärtner,
15 Wenn er die Hecken stutzt mit der unermeßlichen Schere.)
Lauter Nichts ist sein Tun und voll von törichten Grillen:

Wenn er herniedersteigt vom Gebirg' bei nächtlicher Weile,
Laut im Gespräch mit sich selbst, und oft ingrimmigen
    Herzens
Weg- und Meilenzeiger mit *einem* gemessenen Tritt knickt
20 (Denn die hasset er bis auf den Tod, unbilligerweise),
Oder auch wenn er zur Winterzeit ins beschneiete Blachfeld
Oft sich der Länge nach streckt und, aufgestanden, an
    seinem
Konterfei sich ergötzt, mit bergerschütterndem Lachen.

Aber nun lag er einmal mittags in seiner Behausung,
25 Seinen geliebtesten Fraß zu verdau'n, saftstrotzende Rüben,
Zu dem geräucherten Speck, den die Bauern ihm bringen
    vertragsweis;
Plötzlich erfüllet wonniger Glanz die Wände der Höhle:
Lolegrin stand vor ihm, der liebliche Götterjüngling,
Welcher ein Lustigmacher bestellt ist seligen Göttern,
30 (Sonst nur auf Orplid gesehn, denn andre Lande vermied er),
Weylas schalkischer Sohn, mit dem Narrenkranz um die
    Schläfe,
Zierlich aus blauen Glocken und Küchenschelle geflochten.
Er nun red'te den Ruhenden an mit trüglichem Ernste:
„Suckelborst, sicherer Mann, sei gegrüßt und höre vertrau-
    lich,
35 Was die Himmlischen dir durch meine Sendung entbieten!
— Sämtlich ehren sie deinen Verstand und gute Gemütsart,
So wie deine Geburt: es war dein Vater ein Halbgott,
Und desgleichen auch hielten sie dich stets; aber in *einem*
Bist du ihnen nicht recht; das sollst du jetzo vernehmen.
40 Bleibe nur, Lieber, getrost so liegen! ich setze bescheiden
Mich auf den Absatzrand hier deines würdigen Stiefels,
Der wie ein Felsblock ragt, und unschwer bin ich zu tragen.

Siehe! Serachadan zeugete dich mit der Riesenkröte,
Seine unsterbliche Kraft in ihrem Leibe verschließend,
45 Da sie noch lebend war; doch gleich nach ihrer Empfängnis
Ward sie verwandelt in Stein und hauchte dein Vater den
    Geist aus.
Aber du schliefest im Mutterleib neun Monde und drüber,
Denn im zehnten kamen die großen Wasser auf Erden;
Vierzig Tage lang strömte der Regen und vierzig Nächte
50 Auf die sündige Welt, so Tiere wie Menschen ersäufend;

Eine einzige See war über die Lande ergossen,
Über Gebirg' und Tal, und deckte die wolkigen Gipfel.
Doch du lagest zufrieden in deinem Felsen verborgen,
So wie die Auster ruht in festverschlossenen Schalen,
55 Oder des Meeres Preis, die unbezahlbare Perle.
Götter segneten deinen Schlaf mit hohen Gesichten,
Zeigten der Schöpfung Heimliches dir, wie alles geworden:
Erst, wie der Erdball, ganz mit wirkenden Kräften ge-
schwängert,
Einst dem dunkelen Nichts entschwebte zusamt den Ge-
stirnen,
60 Wie mit Gras und Kraut sich zuerst der Boden begrünte,
Wie aus der Erde Milch, so sie hegt im inneren Herzen,
Wurde des Fleisches Gebild', das zarte, darinnen der Geist
wohnt,
Tier- und Menschengeschlecht, denn erdgeboren sind beide.
Zudem sang dir dein Traum der Völker späteste Zukunft
65 So wie der Throne Wechselgeschick und der Könige Taten,
Ja, du sahst den verborgenen Rat der ewigen Götter.
Solches vergönnten sie dir, auf daß du, ein herrlicher Lehrer
Oder ein Seher, die Wahrheit wiederum andern verkündest,
Nicht den Menschen sowohl, die da leben und wandeln auf
Erden —
70 Ihnen ja dient nur wenig zu wissen —, ich meine die Geister
Unten im Schattengefild', die alten Weisen und Helden,
Welche da traurig sitzen und forschen das hohe Verhängnis,
Schweigsam immerdar, des erquicklichen Wortes ent-
behrend.
Aber vergebens harren sie dein, dieweil du ja gänzlich
75 Deines erhabnen Berufs nicht denkst. Laß, Alter, mich offen
Dir gestehen, so, wie du es bisher getrieben, erscheinst du
Weder ein Halbgott noch ein Begeisteter, sondern ein
Schweinpelz.
Greulichem Fraß nachtrachtest du nur und sinnest auf
Unheil:
Steigest des Nachts in den Fluß, bis über die Kniee gestiefelt,
80 Trennest die Bänder los an den Flößen und schleuderst die
Balken
Weit hinein in das Land, den ehrlichen Flößern zum Torten.
Taglang trollest du müßig umher im wilden Gebirge,
Ahmest das Grunzen des Keulers nach und lockest sein
Weibchen,

Greifest, wenn sie nun rennt durch den Busch, die Sau bei
den Ohren,

85 Zwickst die wütende, grausam an ihrem Geschrei dich
weider d.

Siehe, dies wissen wir wohl; denn jegliches sehen die Götter.
Aber du reize sie länger nicht mehr! es möchte dich reuen.
Schmeidige doch ein weniges deine borstige Seele!
Suche zusammen dein Wissen und lichte die rußigen Kam-
mern

90 Deines Gehirns und besinne dich wohl auf alles und jedes,
Was dir geoffenbart; dann nimm den Griffel und zeichn' es
Fein mit Fleiß in ein Buch, damit es daure und bleibe;
Leg' den Toten es aus in der Unterwelt! Sicherlich weißt du
Wohl die Pfade dahin und den Eingang, welcher dich
nicht schreckt,

95 Denn du bist ja der sichere Mann mit den wackeren Stiefeln.
Lieber, und also scheid' ich. Ade! wir sehen uns wieder."

Sprach es, der schelmische Gott, und ließ den Alten alleine.
Der nun war wie verstürzt, und stand ihm fast der Verstand
still.

Halblaut hebt er zu brummen erst an und endlich zu fluchen,

100 Schandbare Worte zumal, gottloseste, nicht zu beschreiben.
Aber nachdem die Galle verraucht war und die Empörung,
Hielt er inne und schwieg; denn jetzo gemahnte der Geist
ihn,

Nicht zu trotzen den Himmlischen, deren doch immer die
Macht ist,

Sondern zu folgen vielmehr. Und alsbald wühlt sein Ge-
danke

105 Rückwärts durch der Jahrtausende Wust, bis tief wo er
selber

Noch ein Ungeborener träumte die Wehen der Schöpfung
(Denn so sagte der Gott und Götter werden nicht lügen);
Aber da deucht es ihm Nacht, dickfinstere; wo er umher-
tappt,

Nirgend ist noch ein Halt und noch kein Nagel geschlagen,

110 Anzuhängen die Wucht der wundersamen Gedanken,
Welche der Gott ihm erregt in seiner erhabenen Seele;
Und so kam er zu nichts und schwitzete wie ein Magister.
Endlich ward ihm geschenkt, daß er flugs dahin sich be-
dachte:

Erst ein Buch sich zu schaffen, ein unbeschriebenes, großes,
115 Seinen Fäusten gerecht und wert des künftigen Inhalts.
Wie er solches erreicht, o Muse, dies hilf mir verkünden!

Längst war die Sonne hinab, und Nacht beherrschte den
        Erdkreis
Seit vier Stunden, da hebt der sichere Mann sich vom Lager,
Setzet den runden Hut auf das Haupt und fasset den Wander-
120 Stab und verlässet die Höhle. Gemächlich steigt er berg-
        aufwärts,
Red't mit sich selber dabei und brummt nach seiner Ge-
        wohnheit.

Aber nun hub sich der Mond auch schon in leuchtender
        Schöne
Rein am Forchenwalde herauf und erhellte die Gegend
Samt der Höhe von Igelsloch, wo nun Suckelborst anlangt.
125 Kaum erst hatte der Wächter die zwölfte Stunde gerufen,
Alles ist ruhig im Dorf und nirgend ein Licht mehr zu sehen,
Nicht in den Kunkelstuben gesellig spinnender Mägdlein,
Nicht am einsamen Stuhle des Webers oder im Wirtshaus,
Mann und Weib im Bette, die Last des Tages verschlafend.

130 Suckelborst tritt nun sacht vor die nächstgelegene Scheuer,
Misset die zween Torflügel, die Höhe sowohl wie die Breite,
Still mit zufriedenem Blick (auch waren sie nicht von den
        kleinsten,
Aber er selbst war größer denn sie, dieweil er ein Riese).
Schloß und Riegel betrachtet er wohl, kneipt dann mit dem
        Finger
135 Ab den Kloben und öffnet das Tor und hebet die Flügel
Leicht aus den Angeln und lehnt an die Wand sie überein-
        ander.
Alsbald schaut er sich um nach des Nachbars Scheuer und
        schreitet
Zu demselben Geschäft und raubet die mächtigen Tore,
Stellt zu den vorigen sie an die Wand, und also fort macht er
140 Weiter im Gäßchen hinauf, bis er dem fünften und sechsten
Bauern auf gleiche Weise die Tenne gelüftet. Am Ende
Überzählt er die Stücke: es waren gerade ein Dutzend
Blätter und fehlte nur noch, daß er mit sauberen Stricken

Hinten die Öhre der Angeln verband, da war es ein Schreib-
buch,
145 Gar ein stattliches; doch dies blieb ein Geschäft für daheime.
Also nimmt er es unter den Arm, das Werk, und trollt sich.

Unterdes war aufschauernd vom Schlaf der schnarchenden
Bauern
Einer erwacht und hörte des schwer Entwandelnden
Fußtritt.
Hastig entrauscht er dem Lager und stößt am niedrigen
Fenster
150 Rasch den Schieber zurück und horcht und sieht mit Ent-
setzen
Rings im mondlichen Dorf der Scheuern finstere Rachen
Offen stehn; da fährt er voll Angst in die lederne Hose
(Beide Füße verkehrt, den linken macht er zum rechten),
Rüttelt sein Weib und redet zu ihr die eifrigen Worte:
155 „Käthe, steh auf! Der sichere Mann — ich hab' ihn ver-
nommen —
Hat wie der Feind im Flecken hantiert und die Scheuern
geplündert!
Schau im Hause mir nach und im Stall! ich laufe zum
Schulzen."
Also stürmt er hinaus. Doch tut er selber im Hof erst
Noch einen Blick in die Ställe, ob auch sein Vieh noch vor-
handen;
160 Aber da fehlte kein Schweif, und es muht ihm entgegen die
Schecke,
Meint, es wär' Fütternszeit; er aber enteilt in die Gasse,
Klopft unterwegs dem Büttel am Laden und ruft ihm das
Wort zu:
„Michel heraus! mach Lärm! Der sichere Mann hat den
Flecken
Heimgesucht und die Scheuern erbrochen und übel ge-
wirtschaft't!"
165 Solches noch redend, hinweg schon lief er und weckte den
Schultheiß,
Weckte den Bürgermeister und andere seiner Gefreund'te.
Alsbald wurden die Straßen lebendig, es staunten die
Männer,
Stießen Verwünschungen aus, im Chor lamentierten die
Weiber,

Jeder durchmusterte seinen Besitz, und wenig getröstet,
170 Als kein größerer Schaden herauskam, fielen mit Unrecht
Über den Wächter die grimmigsten her und schrien: „Du
Schlafratz!
Du keinnütziger Tropf!" und ballten die bäurischen Fäuste,
Ihn zu bleuen, und nahmen auch nur mit Mühe Vernunft an.
Endlich zerstreuten sie sich zur Ruhe; doch stellte der
Schultheiß
175 Wachen noch aus für den Fall, daß der Unhold noch einmal
käme.

Suckelborst hatte derweil schon wieder die Höhle ge-
wonnen,
Welche von vorn gar weit und hoch in den Felsen sich
wölbte.
Duftende Kiefern umschatteten, riesige, dunkel den Ein-
gang.
Hier denn leget er nieder die ungeheueren Tore
180 Und sich selber dazu, des goldenen Schlafes genießend.

Aber sobald die Sonne nur zwischen den Bäumen herein-
schien,
Gleich an die Arbeit machet er sich, die Tore zu heften.
Saubere Stricke schon lagen bereit, gestohlene freilich;
Und er ordnet die Blätter mit sinnigen Blicken und füget
185 Vorn und hinten zur Decke die schönsten (sie waren des
Schulzen,
Künstlich über das Kreuz mit roten Leisten beschlagen).
Aber auf einmal jetzt, in des stattlichen Werkes Betrachtung,
Wächst ihm der Geist, und er nimmt die mächtige Kohle
vom Boden,
Legt vor das offene Buch sich nieder und schreibet aus
Kräften
190 Striche, so grad' wie krumm, in unnachsagbaren Sprachen,
Kratzt und schreibt und brummelt dabei mit zufriedenem
Nachdruck.
Anderthalb Tag' arbeitet er so, kaum gönnet er Zeit sich,
Speise zu nehmen und Trank, bis die letzte Seite gefüllt ist;
Endlich am Schluß denn folgt das Punktum, groß wie ein
Kindskopf.
195 Tief aufschnaufend erhebet er sich, sein Buch zuschmet-
ternd.

Jetzo, nachdem er das Herz sich gestärkt mit reichlicher
    Mahlzeit,
Nimmt er den Hut und den Stock und reiset. Auf einsamen
    Pfaden
Stets gen Mitternacht läuft er, denn dies ist der Weg zu den
    Toten.
Schon mit dem siebenten Morgen erreicht er die finstere
    Pforte.
200 Purpurn streifte soeben die Morgenröte den Himmel,
    Welche den lebenden Menschen das Licht des Tages ver-
    kündet,
Als er hinabwärts stieg, furchtlos, die felsigen Hallen.
Aber er hatte der Stunden noch zweimal zwölfe zu wandeln
Durch der Erde gewundenes Ohr, wo ihn Lolegrin heimlich
205 Führete, bis er die Schatten ersah, die, luftig und schwebend,
    Dämmernde Räume bewohnen, die Bösen sowohl wie die
    Guten.

Vorn bei dem Eingang sammelte sich unliebsames Kehricht
Niederen Volks: trugsinnende Krämer und Kuppler und
    Metzen,
Lausige Dichter dabei und unzählbares Gesindel.
210 Diese, zu schwatzen gewohnt, zu Possen geneigt und zu
    Händeln,
Mühten vergebens sich ab, zu erheben die lispelnde
    Stimme—
Denn hellklingendes Wort ist nicht den Toten verliehen —
Und so winkten sie nur mit heftig bewegter Gebärde,
Stießen und zerrten einander als wie im Gewühle des Jahr-
    markts.
215 Weiter dagegen hinein sah man ruhmwürdige Geister,
    Könige, Helden und Sänger, geschmückt mit ewigem Lor-
    beer.
Ruhig ergingen sie sich und saßen, die einen zusammen,
Andre für sich, und es trennte die weit zerstreueten Gruppen
Hügel und Fels und Gebüsch und die finstere Wand der
    Zypressen.

220 Kaum nun war der sichere Mann in der Pforte erschienen,
    Aufrecht die hohe Gestalt, mit dem Weltbuch unter dem
    Arme,

Sieh, da betraf die Schatten am Eingang tödliches Schrecken.
Auseinander stoben sie all, wie Kinder vom Spielplatz,
Wenn es im Dorfe nun heißt: „Der Hummel ist los! und da
    kommt er!"
225 Doch der sichere Mann, vorschreitend, winkete gnädig
Ringsumher, da kamen sie näher und standen und gafften.

Suckelborst lehnet nunmehr sein mächtiges Manuskriptum
Gegen den niedrigen Hügel, den rundlichen, welchem gen-
    über
Er selbst Platz zu nehmen gedenkt auf moosigem Fels-
    stück.
230 Doch erst leget er Hut und Stock zur Seite bedächtig,
Streicht mit der breiten Hand sich den beißenden Schweiß
    von der Stirne,
Räuspert sich, daß die Hallen ein prasselndes Echo ver-
    senden,
Sitzet nieder sodann und beginnt den erhabenen Vortrag.
Erst, wie der Erdball, ganz mit wirkenden Kräften ge-
    schwängert,
235 Einst dem dunkelen Nichts entschwebte zusamt den Ge-
    stirnen,
Wie mit Gras und Kraut sich zuerst der Boden begrünte,
Wie aus der Erde Milch, so sie hegt im inneren Herzen,
Wurde des Fleisches Gebild, das zarte, darinnen der Geist
    wohnt,
Tier- und Menschengeschlecht; denn erdgeboren sind beide.

240 Solches, nach bestem Verstand und soweit ihn der Dämon
    erleuchtet,
Lehrte der Alte getrost, und still aufhorchten die Schatten.
Aber es hatte der Teufel, das schwarze, gehörnete Scheusal,
Sich aus fremdem Gebiet des unterirdischen Reiches
Unberufen hier eingedrängt, neugierig und boshaft,
245 Wie er wohl manchmal pflegt, wenn er Kundschaft suchet
    und Kurzweil.
Und er stellte sich hinter den Sprechenden, ihn zu verhöh-
    nen,
Schnitt Gesichter und reckte die Zung' und machete Purzel-
Bäum' als ein Aff', und reizte die Seelen beständig zu lachen.
Wohl bemerkt' es der sichere Mann, doch tat er nicht also,
250 Sondern er redete fort, in würdiger Ruhe beharrend.

Indes trieb es der andere nur um desto verwegner,
Schob am Ende den Schwanz, den gewichtigen, langen, dem
    Alten
Sacht in die Hintertasche des Rocks, als wenn es ihn fröre:
Plötzlich da greifet der sichere Mann nach hinten, gewaltig
255 Mit der Rechten erfaßt er den Schweif und reißet ihn schnel-
    lend
Bei der Wurzel heraus, daß es kracht — ein gräßlicher An-
    blick.
Laut auf brüllet der Böse, die Tatzen gedeckt auf die Wunde,
Dreht im rasenden Schmerz wie ein Kreisel sich, schreiend
    und winselnd,
Und schwarz quoll ihm das Blut wie rauchendes Pech aus der
    Wunde;
260 Dann, wie ein Pfeil zur Seite gewandt, mit Schanden en-
    trinnt er
Durch die geschwind eröffnete Gasse der staunenden Seelen,
Denn nach der eigenen Hölle verlangt ihn, wo er zu Haus
    war.
Und man hörte noch weit aus der Ferne des Flüchtigen
    Wehlaut.

Aber es standen die Scharen umher, von Grausen gefesselt,
265 Ehrfurchtsvoll zum sicheren Mann die Augen erhoben.
Dieser hielt noch und wog den wuchtigen Schweif in den
    Händen,
Den bisweilen ein zuckender Schmerz noch leise bewegte.
Sinnend schaut' er ihn an und sprach die prophetischen
    Worte:
„Wie oft tut der sichere Mann dem Teufel ein Leides?
270 Erstlich heute, wie eben geschehn, ihr saht es mit Augen.
Dann ein zweites, ein drittes Mal in der Zeiten Vollendung:
Dreimal rauft der sichere Mann dem Teufel den Schweif aus.
Neu zwar sprosset hervor ihm derselbige, aber nicht ganz
    mehr;
Kürzer gerät er, je um ein Dritteil, bis daß er welket.
275 Gleichermaßen vergeht dem Bösen der Mut und die Stärke,
Kindisch wird er und alt, ein Bettler, von allen verachtet.
Dann wird ein Festtag sein in der Unterwelt und auf der
    Erde;
Aber der sichere Mann wird ein lieber Genosse den Göt-
    tern."

Sprach es, und jetzo legt' er den Schweif in das Buch als ein
    Zeichen,
280 Sorgsam, daß oben noch just der haarige Büschel heraussah,
Denn er gedachte für jetzt nicht weiter zu lehren, und basta
Schmettert er zu den Deckel des ungeheueren Werkes,
Faßt es unter den Arm, nimmt Hut und Stock und empfiehlt
    sich.

Unermeßliches Beifallklatschen des sämtlichen Pöbels
285 Folgte dem Trefflichen nach, bis er ganz in der Pforte
    verschwunden,
Und es rauschte noch lang und tosete freudiger Aufruhr.

Aber Lolegrin hatte, der Gott, das ganze Spektakel
Heimlich mit angesehn und gehört, in Gestalt der Zikade
Auf dem hangenden Zweig der schwarzen Weide sich
    wiegend.
290 Jetzo verließ er den Ort und schwang sich empor zu den
    Göttern,
Ihnen treulich zu melden die Taten des sicheren Mannes
Und das himmlische Mahl mit süßem Gelächter zu würzen.

48. SCHÖN-ROHTRAUT

Wie heißt König Ringangs Töchterlein?
    Rohtraut, Schön-Rohtraut.
Was tut sie denn den ganzen Tag,
Da sie wohl nicht spinnen und nähen mag?
5   Tut fischen und jagen.
O daß ich doch ihr Jäger wär'!
Fischen und Jagen freute mich sehr.
— Schweig stille, mein Herze!

Und über eine kleine Weil',
10   Rohtraut, Schön-Rohtraut,
So dient der Knab' auf Ringangs Schloß
In Jägertracht und hat ein Roß,
    Mit Rohtraut zu jagen.
O daß ich doch ein Königssohn wär'!
15 Rohtraut, Schön-Rohtraut lieb' ich so sehr.
— Schweig stille, mein Herze!

Einsmals sie ruhten am Eichenbaum,
    Da lacht Schön-Rohtraut:
„Was siehst mich an so wunniglich?
20 Wenn du das Herz hast, küsse mich!"
    Ach! erschrak der Knabe!
Doch denket er: „Mir ist's vergunnt",
Und küsset Schön-Rohtraut auf den Mund.
— Schweig stille, mein Herze!

25 Darauf sie ritten schweigend heim,
    Rohtraut, Schön-Rohtraut;
Es jauchzt der Knab' in seinem Sinn:
„Und würdst du heute Kaiserin,
    Mich sollt's nicht kränken!
30 Ihr tausend Blätter im Walde wißt,
Ich hab' Schön-Rohtrauts Mund geküßt!
— Schweig stille, mein Herze!"

49. IM WEINBERG

Droben im Weinberg unter dem blühenden Kirschbaum saß
    ich
Heut einsam, in Gedanken vertieft; es ruhte das Neue
Testament halboffen mir zwischen den Fingern im Schoße,
Klein und zierlich gebunden: (es kam vom treuesten
    Herzen —
5 Ach! du ruhest nun auch, mir unvergessen, im Grabe!)
Lang' so saß ich und blickte nicht auf: mit einem da läßt sich
Mir ein Schmetterling nieder aufs Buch, er hebet und senket
Dunkele Flügel mit schillerndem Blau, er dreht sich und
    wandelt
Hin und her auf dem Rande. Was suchst du, reizender
    Sylphe?
10 Lockte die purpurne Decke dich an, der glänzende Gold-
    schnitt?
Sahst du, getäuscht, im Büchlein die herrlichste Wunder-
    blume?
Oder zogen geheim dich himmlische Kräfte hernieder
Des lebendigen Worts? Ich muß so glauben, denn immer
Weilest du noch wie gebannt und scheinst wie trunken — ich
    staune!
15 Aber von nun an bist du alle Tage gesegnet!

Unverletzlich dein Leib, und es altern dir nimmer die
    Schwingen;
Ja, wohin du künftig die zarten Füße wirst setzen,
Tauet Segen von dir. Jetzt eile hinunter zum Garten,
Welchen das beste der Mädchen besucht am frühesten
    Morgen,
20 Eile zur Lilie du — alsbald wird die Knospe sich öffnen
Unter dir; dann küsse sie tief in den Busen: von Stund an
Göttlich befruchtet, atmet sie Geist und himmlisches Leben.
Wenn die Gute nun kommt, vor den hohen Stengel getreten,
Steht sie befangen, entzückt von paradiesischer Nähe,
25 Ahnungsvoll in den Kelch die liebliche Seele versenkend.

50. DER ALTE TURMHAHN

Idylle

Zu Cleversulzbach im Unterland
Hundertunddreizehn Jahr' ich stand,
Auf dem Kirchenturm, ein guter Hahn,
Als ein Zierat und Wetterfahn'.
5 In Sturm und Wind und Regennacht
Hab' ich allzeit das Dorf bewacht.
Manch falber Blitz hat mich gestreift,
Der Frost mein' roten Kamm bereift,
Auch manchen lieben Sommertag,
10 Da man gern Schatten haben mag,
Hat mir die Sonne unverwandt
Auf meinen goldigen Leib gebrannt.
So ward ich schwarz für Alter ganz,
Und weg ist aller Glitz und Glanz.
15 Da haben sie mich denn zuletzt
Veracht't und schmählich abgesetzt.
Meinthalb! so ist der Welt ihr Lauf,
Jetzt tun sie einen andern 'nauf.
Stolzier', prachtier' und dreh dich nur!
20 Dir macht der Wind noch andre Cour.

Ade, o Tal, du Berg und Tal!
Rebhügel, Wälder allzumal!
Herzlieber Turm und Kirchendach,
Kirchhof und Steglein übern Bach!

25 Du Brunnen, dahin spat und früh
Öchslein springen, Schaf' und Küh',
Hans hinterdrein kommt mit dem Stecken
Und Bastes Evlein mit dem Schecken!
— Ihr Störch' und Schwalben, grobe Spatzen,
30 Euch soll ich nimmer hören schwatzen!
Lieb deucht mir jedes Drecklein itzt,
Damit ihr ehrlich mich beschmitzt.
Ade, Hochwürden, Ihr, Herr Pfarr,
Schulmeister auch, du armer Narr!
35 Aus ist, was mich gefreut so lang',
Geläut' und Orgel, Sang und Klang.

Von meiner Höh' so sang ich dort
Und hätt' noch lang' gesungen fort,
Da kam so ein krummer Teufelshöcker,
40 Ich schätz', es war der Schieferdecker,
Packt mich, kriegt nach manch hartem Stoß
Mich richtig von der Stange los.
Mein alt preßhafter Leib schier brach,
Da er mit mir fuhr ab dem Dach
45 Und bei den Glocken schnurrt' hinein.
Die glotzten sehr verwundert drein;
Regt' ihnen doch weiter nicht den Mut,
Dachten eben, wir hangen gut.

Jetzt tät man mich mit altem Eisen
50 Dem Meister Hufschmied überweisen;
Der zahlt zween Batzen und meint Wunder,
Wieviel es wär' für solchen Plunder.
Und also ich selben Mittag
Betrübt vor seiner Hütte lag.
55 Ein Bäumlein — es war Maienzeit —
Schneeweiße Blüten auf mich streut,
Hühner gackeln um mich her,
Unachtend, was das für ein Vetter wär'.
Da geht mein Pfarrherr nun vorbei,
60 Grüßt den Meister und lächelt: „Ei,
Wär's so weit mit uns, armer Hahn?
Andrees, was fangt Ihr mit ihm an?
Ihr könnt ihn weder sieden noch braten,
Mir aber müßt' es schlimm geraten,

65 Einen alten Kirchendiener gut
Nicht zu nehmen in Schutz und Hut.
Kommt! tragt ihn mir gleich vor ins Haus,
Trinket ein kühl' Glas Wein mit aus!"

Der rußig' Lümmel, schnell bedacht,
70 Nimmt mich vom Boden auf und lacht.
Es fehlt' nicht viel, so tat ich frei
Gen Himmel einen Freudenschrei.
Im Pfarrhaus, ob dem fremden Gast
War groß und klein erschrocken fast;
75 Bald aber in jedem Angesicht
Ging auf ein rechtes Freudenlicht.
Frau, Magd und Knecht, Mägdlein und Buben
Den großen Göckel in der Stuben
Mit siebenfacher Stimmen Schall
80 Begrüßen, begucken, betasten all'.
Der Gottesmann drauf mildiglich
Mit eignen Händen trägt er mich
Nach seinem Zimmer, Stiegen auf,
Nachpolteret der ganze Hauf'.

85 Hier wohnt der Frieden auf der Schwell'.
In den geweißten Wänden hell
Sogleich empfing mich sondre Luft,
Bücher- und Gelehrtenduft,
Gerani- und Resedaschmack,
90 Auch ein Rüchlein Rauchtabak.
(Dies war mir all noch unbekannt.)
Ein alter Ofen aber stand
In der Ecke linker Hand.
Recht als ein Turm tät er sich strecken
95 Mit seinem Gipfel bis zur Decken,
Mit Säulwerk, Blumwerk, kraus und spitz —
O anmutsvoller Ruhesitz!
Zuöberst auf dem kleinen Kranz
Der Schmied mich auf ein Stänglein pflanzt'.

100 Betrachtet' mir das Werk genau!
Mir deucht's ein ganzer Münsterbau,
Mit Schildereien wohl geziert,
Mit Reimen christlich ausstaffiert.
Davon vernahm ich manches Wort,

105 Dieweil der Ofen ein guter Hort
Für Kind und Kegel und alte Leut',
Zu plaudern, wann es wind't und schneit.

Hier seht ihr seitwärts auf der Platten
Eines Bischofs Krieg mit Mäus' und Ratten,
110 Mitten im Rheinstrom sein Kastell.
Das Ziefer kommt geschwommen schnell,
Die Knecht' nichts richten mit Waffen und Wehr,
Der Schwänze werden immer mehr.
Viel Tausend gleich in dicken Haufen.
115 Frech an der Mauer auf sie laufen,
Fallen dem Pfaffen in sein Gemach;
Sterben muß er mit Weh und Ach,
Von den Tieren aufgefressen,
Denn er mit Meineid sich vermessen.
120 — Sodann König Belsazers seinen Schmaus,
Weiber und Spielleut', Saus und Braus;
Zu großem Schrecken an der Wand
Rätsel schreibt eines Geistes Hand.
— Zuletzt da vorne stellt sich für
125 Sara lauschend an der Tür,
Als der Herr mit Abraham
Vor seiner Hütte zu reden kam
Und ihme einen Sohn versprach.
Sara sich Lachens nicht entbrach,
130 Weil sie beide schon sehr hoch betaget.
Der Herr vernimmt es wohl und fraget:
„Wie, lachet Sara? glaubt sie nicht,
Was der Herr will, leicht geschicht?"
Das Weib hinwieder Flausen machet,
135 Spricht: „Ich habe nicht gelachet."
Das war nun wohl gelogen fast,
Der Herr es doch passieren laßt,
Weil sie nicht leugt aus arger List,
Auch eine Patriarchin ist.

140 Seit daß ich hier bin, dünket mir
Die Winterszeit die schönste schier.
Wie sanft ist aller Tage Fluß
Bis zum geliebten Wochenschluß!
— Freitag zu Nacht, noch um die Neune,

145 Bei seiner Lampen Trost alleine,
      Mein Herr fangt an sein Predigtlein
      Studieren; anderst mag's nicht sein.
      Eine Weil' am Ofen brütend steht,
      Unruhig hin und dannen geht:
150 Sein Text ihm schon die Adern reget;
      Drauf er sein Werk zu Faden schläget.
      Inmittelst einmal auch etwan
      Hat er ein Fenster aufgetan —
      Ah, Sternenlüfteschwall wie rein
155 Mit Haufen dringet zu mir ein!
      Den Verrenberg ich schimmern seh',
      Den Schäferbühel dick mit Schnee!

      Zu schreiben endlich er sich setzet,
      Ein Blättlein nimmt, die Feder netzet,
160 Zeichnet sein Alpha und sein O
      Über dem Exordio.
      Und ich von meinem Postament
      Kein Aug' ab meinem Herrlein wend';
      Seh', wie er, mit Blicken steif ins Licht,
165 Sinnt, prüfet jedes Worts Gewicht,
      Einmal sacht eine Prise greifet,
      Vom Docht den roten Butzen streifet;
      Auch dann und wann zieht er vor sich
      Ein Sprüchlein an vernehmentlich,
170 So ich mit vorgerecktem Kopf
      Begierlich bringe gleich zu Kropf.
      Gemachsam kämen wir also
      Bis Anfang Applicatio.
      Indes der Wächter Elfe schreit.
175 Mein Herr denkt: Es ist Schlafenszeit,
      Ruckt seinen Stuhl und nimmt das Licht.
      — „Gut' Nacht, Herr Pfarr!" — Er hört es nicht.

      Im Finstern wär' ich denn allein;
      Das ist mir eben keine Pein.
180 Ich hör' in der Registratur
      Erst eine Weil' die Totenuhr,
      Lache den Marder heimlich aus,
      Der scharrt sich müd' am Hühnerhaus;
      Windweben um das Dächlein stieben;

185 Ich höre, wie im Wald da drüben —
Man heißet es im Vogeltrost —
Der grimmig' Winter sich erbost,
Ein Eichlein spalt't jähling mit Knallen,
Eine Buche, daß die Täler schallen.
190 — Du meine Güt', da lobt man sich
So frommen Ofen dankbarlich!
Er wärmelt halt die Nacht so hin,
Es ist ein wahrer Segen drin.
— Jetzt, denk' ich, sind wohl hie und dort
195 Spitzbuben aus auf Raub und Mord;
Denk', was eine schöne Sach' es ist,
Brave Schloß und Riegel zu jeder Frist,
Was ich wollt' machen herentgegen,
Wenn ich eine Leiter hört' anlegen,
200 Und sonst was so Gedanken sind;
Ein warmes Schweißlein mir entrinnt.
Um zwei, gottlob! und um die drei
Glänzet empor ein Hahnenschrei,
Um fünfe mit der Morgenglocken
205 Mein Herz sich hebet unerschrocken,
Ja voller Freuden auf es springt,
Als der Wächter endlich singt:
„Wohlauf, im Namen Jesu Christ!
Der helle Tag erschienen ist."

210 Ein Stündlein drauf, wenn mir die Sporen
Bereits ein wenig steif gefroren,
Rasselt die Lis' im Ofen, brummt,
Bis 's Feuer angeht, saust und summt.
Dann von der Küch' 'rauf, gar nicht übel,
215 Die Supp' ich wittre, Schmalz und Zwiebel.
Endlich, gewaschen und geklärt,
Mein Herr sich frisch zur Arbeit kehrt.

Am Samstag muß ein Pfarrer fein
Daheim in seiner Klause sein,
220 Nicht visiteln, herumkutschieren,
Seine Faß einbrennen, sonst hantieren.
Meiner hat selten solch' Gelust.
Einmal — ihr sagt's nicht weiter just —
Zimmert' er den ganzen Nachmittag

225 Dem Fritz an einem Meisenschlag
    Dort an dem Tisch und schwatzt' und schmaucht',
    Mich alten Tropf kurzweilt' es auch.

    Jetzt ist der liebe Sonntag da,
    Es läut't zur Kirchen fern und nah.
230 Man orgelt schon: mir wird dabei,
    Als säß' ich in der Sakristei.
    Es ist kein Mensch im ganzen Haus;
    Ein Mücklein hör' ich, eine Maus.
    Die Sonne sich ins Fenster schleicht,
235 Zwischen die Kaktusstöck' hinstreicht
    Zum kleinen Pult von Nußbaumholz,
    Eines alten Schreinermeisters Stolz;
    Beschaut sich, was da liegt umher,
    Konkordanz und Kinderlehr',
240 Oblatenschachtel, Amtssigill,
    Im Dintenfaß sich spiegeln will,
    Zuteuerst Sand und Grus besicht,
    Sich an dem Federmesser sticht
    Und gleitet übern Armstuhl frank
245 Hinüber an den Bücherschrank.
    Da stehn in Pergament und Leder
    Vornan die frommen Schwabenväter:
    Andreä, Bengel, Rieger zween,
    Samt *Oetinger* sind da zu sehn.
250 Wie sie die goldnen Namen liest,
    Noch goldener ihr Mund sie küßt,
    Wie sie rührt an *Hillers* Harfenspiel —
    Horch! klingt es nicht? so fehlt nicht viel.

    Inmittelst läuft ein Spinnlein zart
255 An mir hinauf nach seiner Art
    Und hängt sein Netz, ohn' erst zu fragen,
    Mir zwischen Schnabel auf und Kragen.
    Ich rühr' mich nicht aus meiner Ruh',
    Schau' ihm eine ganze Weile zu;
260 Darüber ist es wohl geglückt,
    Daß ich ein wenig eingenickt. —
    Nun sagt, ob es in Dorf und Stadt
    Ein alter Kirchhahn besser hat?

    Ein Wunsch im stillen dann und wann

265 Kommt einen freilich wohl noch an.
Im Sommer stünd' ich gern da draus
Bisweilen auf dem Taubenhaus,
Wo dicht dabei der Garten blüht,
Man auch ein Stück vom Flecken sieht.
270 Dann in der schönen Winterzeit,
Als zum Exempel eben heut';
Ich sag' es grad' — da haben wir
Gar einen wackern Schlitten hier,
Grün, gelb und schwarz; er ward verwichen
275 Erst wieder sauber angestrichen;
Vorn auf dem Bogen brüstet sich
Ein fremder Vogel hoffärtig —
Wenn man mich etwas putzen wollt',
Nicht, daß es drum viel kosten sollt',
280 Ich stünd' so gut dort als wie der
Und machet niemand nicht Unehr'!
— Narr! denk' ich wieder, du hast dein Teil!
Willst du noch jetzo werden geil?
Mich wundert, ob dir nicht gefiel,
285 Daß man, der Welt zum Spott und Ziel,
Deinen warmen Ofen gar zuletzt
Mitsamt dir auf die Läufe setzt',
Daß auf dem G'sims da um dich säß'
Mann, Weib und Kind, der ganze Käs'!
290 Du alter Scherb, schämst du dich nicht,
Auf Eitelkeit zu sein erpicht?
Geh in dich, nimm dein Ende wahr!
Wirst nicht noch einmal hundert Jahr'.

51. WALDPLAGE

Im Walde deucht mir alles miteinander schön,
Und nichts Mißliebiges darin, so vielerlei
Er hegen mag; es krieche zwischen Gras und Moos
Am Boden oder jage reißend durchs Gebüsch,
5 Es singe oder kreische von den Gipfeln hoch
Und hacke mit dem Schnabel in der Fichte Stamm,
Daß lieblich sie ertönet durch den ganzen Saal.
Ja machte je sich irgend etwas unbequem,
Verdrießt es nicht, zu suchen einen andern Sitz,
10 Der schöner bald, der allerschönste dich bedünkt.

Ein einzig Übel aber hat der Wald für mich,
Ein grausames und unausweichliches beinah'.
Sogleich beschreib' ich dieses Scheusal, daß ihr's kennt;
Noch kennt ihr's kaum und merkt es nicht, bis unversehns
15 Die Hand euch und, noch schrecklicher, die Wange schmerzt.
Geflügelt kommt es, säuselnd, fast unhörbarlich;
Auf Füßen, zweimal dreien, ist es hoch gestellt
(Deswegen ich, in Versen es zu schmähen, auch
Den klassischen Senarium mit Fug erwählt);
20 Und wie es anfliegt, augenblicklich lässet es
Den langen Rüssel senkrecht in die zarte Haut;
Erschrocken schlagt ihr schnell darnach, jedoch umsonst,
Denn, graziöser Wendung, schon entschwebet es.
Und alsobald, entzündet von dem raschen Gift,
25 Schwillt euch die Hand zum ungestalten Kissen auf
Und juckt und spannt und brennet zum Verzweifeln euch
Viel' Stunden, ja zuweilen noch den dritten Tag.
So unter meiner Lieblingsfichte saß ich jüngst —
Zur Lehne wie gedrechselt für den Rücken, steigt
30 Zwiestämmig, nah' dem Boden, sie als Gabel auf —
Den Dichter lesend, den ich jahrelang vergaß:
An Fanny singt er, Cidli und den Züricher See,
Die frühen Gräber und des Rheines goldnen Wein
(O, sein Gestade brütet jenes Greuels auch
35 Ein größeres Geschlechte noch und schlimmres aus;
Ich kenn' es wohl, doch höflicher dem Gaste war's.) —
Nun aber hatte geigend schon ein kleiner Trupp
Mich ausgewittert, den geruhig Sitzenden;
Mir um die Schläfe tanzet er in Lüsternheit.
40 Ein Stich! der erste! er empört die Galle schon.
Zerstreuten Sinnes immer schiel' ich übers Blatt.
Ein zweiter macht, ein dritter mich zum Rasenden.
Das holde Zwillings-Nymphen-Paar des Fichtenbaums
Vernahm da Worte, die es nicht bei mir gesucht;
45 Zuletzt geboten sie mir flüsternd Mäßigung:
Wo nicht, so sollt ich meiden ihren Ruhbezirk.
Beschämt gehorcht' ich, sinnend still auf Grausamtat.
Ich hielt geöffnet auf der flachen Hand das Buch,
Das schwebende Geziefer, wie sich eines naht',
50 Mit raschem Klapp zu töten. Ha, da kommt schon eins!
„Du fliehst! o bleibe, eile nicht, Gedankenfreund!"
(Dem hohen Mond rief jener Dichter zu dies Wort.)

Patsch! Hab' ich dich, Canaille, oder hab' ich nicht?
Und hastig — denn schon hatte meine Mordbegier
55 Zum stillen Wahnsinn sich verirrt, zum kleinlichen —
Begierig blättr' ich: ja, da liegst du plattgedrückt,
Bevor du stachst, nun aber stichst du nimmermehr,
Du zierlich Langgebeinetes, Jungfräuliches!
— Also, nicht achtend eines schönen Buchs Verderb,
60 Trieb ich erheitert lange noch die schnöde Jagd,
Unglücklich oft, doch öfter glücklichen Erfolgs.

So mag es kommen, daß ein künft'ger Leser wohl
Einmal in Klopstocks Oden, nicht ohn' einiges
Verwundern, auch etwelcher Schnaken sich erfreut.

52. AUF EINER WANDERUNG

In ein freundliches Städtchen tret' ich ein,
In den Straßen liegt roter Abendschein.
Aus einem offnen Fenster eben,
Über den reichsten Blumenflor
5 Hinweg, hört man Goldglockentöne schweben,
Und *eine* Stimme scheint ein Nachtigallenchor,
Daß die Blüten beben,
Daß die Lüfte leben,
Daß in höherem Rot die Rosen leuchten vor.

10 Lang' hielt ich staunend, lustbeklommen.
Wie ich hinaus vors Tor gekommen,
Ich weiß es wahrlich selber nicht.
Ach hier, wie liegt die Welt so licht!
Der Himmel wogt in purpurnem Gewühle,
15 Rückwärts die Stadt in goldnem Rauch;
Wie rauscht der Erlenbach, wie rauscht im Grund die Mühle!
Ich bin wie trunken, irrgeführt —
O Muse, du hast mein Herz berührt
Mit einem Liebeshauch!

53. AUF EINE CHRISTBLUME

I

Tochter des Walds, du Lilienverwandte,
So lang' von mir gesuchte, unbekannte,

Im fremden Kirchhof, öd' und winterlich,
Zum erstenmal, o schöne, find' ich dich!

5   Von welcher Hand gepflegt du hier erblühtest,
Ich weiß es nicht, noch wessen Grab du hütest;
Ist es ein Jüngling, so geschah ihm Heil,
Ist's eine Jungfrau, lieblich fiel ihr Teil.

Im nächt'gen Hain, von Schneelicht überbreitet,
10 Wo fromm das Reh an dir vorüberweidet,
Bei der Kapelle, am krystallnen Teich,
Dort sucht' ich deiner Heimat Zauberreich.

Schön bist du, Kind des Mondes, nicht der Sonne;
Dir wäre tödlich andrer Blumen Wonne,
15 Dich nährt, den keuschen Leib voll Reif und Duft,
Himmlischer Kälte balsamsüße Luft.

In deines Busens goldner Fülle gründet
Ein Wohlgeruch, der sich nur kaum verkündet;
So duftete, berührt von Engelshand,
20 Der benedeiten Mutter Brautgewand.

Dich würden, mahnend an das heil'ge Leiden,
Fünf Purpurtropfen schön und einzig kleiden:
Doch kindlich zierst du, um die Weihnachtzeit,
Lichtgrün mit einem Hauch dein weißes Kleid.

25 Der Elfe, der in mitternächt'ger Stunde
Zum Tanze geht im lichterhellen Grunde,
Vor deiner mystischen Glorie steht er scheu
Neugierig still von fern und huscht vorbei.

II

Im Winterboden schläft, ein Blumenkeim,
30 Der Schmetterling, der einst um Busch und Hügel
In Frühlingsnächten wiegt den samtnen Flügel;
Nie soll er kosten deinen Honigseim.

Wer aber weiß, ob nicht sein zarter Geist,
Wenn jede Zier des Sommers hingesunken,
35 Dereinst, von deinem leisen Dufte trunken,
Mir unsichtbar, dich blühende umkreist?

54. AN WILHELM HARTLAUB

Durchs Fenster schien der helle Mond herein;
Du saßest am Klavier im Dämmerschein,
Versankst im Traumgewühl der Melodie'n,
Ich folgte dir an schwarzen Gründen hin,
5 Wo der Gesang versteckter Quellen klang,
Gleich Kinderstimmen, die der Wind verschlang.

Doch plötzlich war dein Spiel wie umgewandt,
Nur blauer Himmel schien noch ausgespannt,
Ein jeder Ton ein lang' gehaltnes Schweigen.
10 Da fing das Firmament sich an zu neigen,
Und jäh daran herab der Sterne selig Heer
Glitt rieselnd in ein goldig Nebelmeer,
Bis Tropf' um Tropfen hell darin zerging,
Die alte Nacht den öden Raum umfing.

15 Und als du neu ein fröhlich Leben wecktest,
Die Finsternis mit jungem Lichte schrecktest,
War ich schon weit hinweg mit Sinn und Ohr,
Zuletzt warst du es selbst, in den ich mich verlor;
Mein Herz durchzückt' mit eins ein Freudenstrahl:
20 Dein ganzer Wert erschien mir auf einmal.
So wunderbar empfand ich es, so neu,
Daß noch bestehe Freundeslieb' und Treu',
Daß uns so sichrer Gegenwart Genuß
Zusammenhält in Lebensüberfluß!

25 Ich sah dein hingesenktes Angesicht
Im Schatten halb und halb im klaren Licht;
Du ahntest nicht, wie mir der Busen schwoll,
Wie mir das Auge brennend überquoll.
Du endigtest; ich schwieg. — Ach, warum ist doch eben
30 Dem höchsten Glück kein Laut des Danks gegeben?

Da tritt dein Töchterchen mit Licht herein:
Ein ländlich Mahl versammelt groß und klein,
Vom nahen Kirchturm schallt das Nachtgeläut',
Verklingend so des Tages Lieblichkeit.

55. DIE SCHÖNE BUCHE

Ganz verborgen im Wald kenn' ich ein Plätzchen, da stehet
　　Eine Buche, man sieht schöner im Bilde sie nicht.
Rein und glatt, in gediegenem Wuchs erhebt sie sich einzeln,
　　Keiner der Nachbarn rührt ihr an den seidenen Schmuck.
5 Rings, so weit sein Gezweig' der stattliche Baum ausbreitet,
　　Grünet der Rasen, das Aug' still zu erquicken, umher;
Gleich nach allen Seiten umzirkt er den Stamm in der Mitte;
　　Kunstlos schuf die Natur selber dies liebliche Rund.
Zartes Gebüsch umkränzet es erst; hochstämmige Bäume,
10　　Folgend in dichtem Gedräng', wehren dem himmlischen
　　　　Blau.
Neben der dunkleren Fülle des Eichbaums wieget die Birke
　　Ihr jungfräuliches Haupt schüchtern im goldenen Licht.
Nur wo, verdeckt vom Felsen, der Fußsteig jäh sich hinab-
　　　　schlingt,
　　Lässet die Hellung mich ahnen das offene Feld.
15 — Als ich unlängst einsam, von neuen Gestalten des Sommers
　　Ab dem Pfade gelockt, dort in Gebüsch mich verlor,
Führt' ein freundlicher Geist, des Hains auflauschende Gott-
　　　　heit,
　　Hier mich zum erstenmal, plötzlich, den Staunenden, ein.
Welch Entzücken! Es war um die hohe Stunde des Mittags,
20　　Lautlos alles, es schwieg selber der Vogel im Laub.
Und ich zauderte noch, auf den zierlichen Teppich zu treten;
　　Festlich empfing er den Fuß, leise beschritt ich ihn nur.
Jetzo, gelehnt an den Stamm (er trägt sein breites Gewölbe
　　Nicht zu hoch), ließ ich rundum die Augen ergehn,
25 Wo den beschatteten Kreis die feurig strahlende Sonne,
　　Fast gleich messend umher, säumte mit blendendem
　　　　Rand.
Aber ich stand und rührte mich nicht; dämonischer Stille,
　　Unergründlicher Ruh' lauschte mein innerer Sinn.
Eingeschlossen mit dir in diesem sonnigen Zauber-
30　　Gürtel, o Einsamkeit, fühlt' ich und dachte nur dich!

56. FRÜH IM WAGEN

Es graut vom Morgenreif
In Dämmerung das Feld,

Da schon ein blasser Streif
Den fernen Ost erhellt;

5 Man sieht im Lichte bald
Den Morgenstern vergehn,
Und doch am Fichtenwald
Den vollen Mond noch stehn:

So ist mein scheuer Blick,
10 Den schon die Ferne drängt,
Noch in das Schmerzensglück
Der Abschiedsnacht versenkt.

Dein blaues Auge steht,
Ein dunkler See, vor mir,
15 Dein Kuß, dein Hauch umweht,
Dein Flüstern mich noch hier.

An deinem Hals begräbt
Sich weinend mein Gesicht,
Und Purpurschwärze webt
20 Mir vor dem Auge dicht.

Die Sonne kommt; — sie scheucht
Den Traum hinweg im Nu,
Und von den Bergen streicht
Ein Schauer auf mich zu.

57. ABREISE

Fertig schon zur Abfahrt steht der Wagen,
Und das Posthorn bläst zum letzten Male.
Sagt, wo bleibt der vierte Mann so lange?
Ruft ihn, soll er nicht dahinten bleiben!
5 — Indes fällt ein rascher Sommerregen;
Eh' man hundert zählt, ist er vorüber;
Fast zu kurz, den heißen Staub zu löschen;
Doch auch diese Letzung ist willkommen.
Kühlung füllt und Wohlgeruch den weiten
10 Platz, und an den Häusern ringsum öffnet
Sich ein Blumenfenster um das andre.

Endlich kommt der junge Mann. Geschwinde!
Eingestiegen! — Und fort rollt der Wagen.
Aber sehet, auf dem nassen Pflaster
15 Vor dem Posthaus, wo er stillgehalten,
Läßt er einen trocknen Fleck zurücke,
Lang und breit, sogar die Räder sieht man
Angezeigt und wo die Pferde standen.
Aber dort in jenem hübschen Hause,
20 Drin der Jüngling sich so lang' verweilte,
Steht ein Mädchen hinterm Fensterladen,
Blicket auf die weiß gelaßne Stelle,
Hält ihr Tüchlein vors Gesicht und weinet.
Mag es ihr so ernst sein? Ohne Zweifel;
25 Doch der Jammer wird nicht lange währen:
Mädchenaugen, wißt ihr, trocknen hurtig,
Und eh' auf dem Markt die Steine wieder
Alle hell geworden von der Sonne,
Könnet ihr den Wildfang lachen hören.

58. AM RHEINFALL

Halte dein Herz, o Wanderer, fest in gewaltigen Händen!
    Mir entstürzte vor Lust zitternd das meinige fast.
Rastlos donnernde Massen auf donnernde Massen geworfen,
    Ohr und Auge, wohin retten sie sich im Tumult?
5 Wahrlich, den eigenen Wutschrei hörete nicht der Gigant hier,
    Läg' er vom Himmel gestürzt, unten am Felsen ge-
    krümmt!
Rosse der Götter, im Schwung, eins über dem Rücken des
    andern,
    Stürmen herunter und streu'n silberne Mähnen umher;
Herrliche Leiber, unzählbare, folgen sich, nimmer dieselben,
10   Ewig dieselben — wer wartet das Ende wohl aus?
Angst umzieht dir den Busen mit eins, und, *wie* du es denkest,
    Über das Haupt stürzt dir krachend das Himmelsge-
    wölb'!

59. AUF EINE LAMPE

Noch unverrückt, o schöne Lampe, schmückest du,
An leichten Ketten zierlich aufgehangen hier,
Die Decke des nun fast vergeßnen Lustgemachs.

Auf deiner weißen Marmorschale, deren Rand
5   Der Efeukranz von goldengrünem Erz umflicht,
Schlingt fröhlich eine Kinderschar den Ringelreih'n.
Wie reizend alles! lachend, und ein sanfter Geist
Des Ernstes doch ergossen um die ganze Form —
Ein Kunstgebild' der echten Art. Wer achtet sein?
10 Was aber schön ist, selig scheint es in ihm selbst.

60. NEUE LIEBE

Kann auch ein Mensch des andern auf der Erde
Ganz, wie er möchte, sein?
— In langer Nacht bedacht' ich mir's und mußte sagen,
           Nein!

So kann ich niemands heißen auf der Erde,
5 Und niemand wäre mein?
— Aus Finsternissen hell in mir aufzückt ein Freuden-
           schein:

Sollt' ich mit Gott nicht können sein,
So wie ich möchte, Mein und Dein?
Was hielte mich, daß ich's nicht heute werde?

10 Ein süßes Schrecken geht durch mein Gebein!
Mich wundert, daß es mir ein Wunder wollte sein,
Gott selbst zu eigen haben auf der Erde!

61. HÄUSLICHE SZENE

*Schlafzimmer. Präzeptor Ziborius und seine junge Frau. Das
Licht ist gelöscht.*

„Schläfst du schon, Rike?" — „Noch nicht." — „Sag'! hast
    du denn heut die Kukumern
    Eingemacht?" — „Ja." — „Und wieviel nahmst du mir
    Essig dazu?" —
„Nicht zwei völlige Maß." — „Wie? fast zwei Maß? Und
    von welchem

Krug? von dem kleinern doch nicht, links vor dem
 Fenster am Hof?" —
5 „Freilich." — „Verwünscht! So darf ich die Probe nun noch
 einmal machen,
Eben indem ich gehofft, schon das Ergebnis zu sehn!
Konntest du mich nicht fragen?" — „Du warst in der
 Schule". — „Nicht warten?" —
„Lieber, zu lange bereits lagen die Gurken mir da." —
„Unlängst sagt' ich dir: nimm von Numero 7 zum Haus-
 brauch" —
10 „Ach, wer behielte denn stets alle die Zahlen im
 Kopf!" —
„Sieben behält sich doch wohl! nichts leichter behalten als
 sieben!
Groß, mit arabischer Schrift, hält es der Zettel dir
 vor." —
„Aber du wechselst den Ort nach der Sonne von Fenster zu
 Fenster
Täglich, die Küche pressiert oft, und ich suche mich
 blind.
15 Bester, dein Essiggebräu, fast will es mich endlich ver-
 drießen.
Ruhig, obgleich mit Not, trug ich so manches bis jetzt.
Daß du im Waschhaus dich einrichtetest, wo es an Raum
 fehlt,
Destillierest und brennst, schien mir das äußerste schon.
Nicht gern sah ich vom Stockbrett erst durch Kolben und
 Krüge
20 Meine Reseden verdrängt, Rosen und Sommerlevkoi'n,
Aber nun stehen ums Haus her rings vor jeglichem Fenster,
 Halb gekleidet in Stroh, gläserne Bäuche gereiht;
Mir auf dem Herd stehn viere zum Hindernis, selber im
 Rauchfang
Hängt so ein Untier jetzt, wieder ein neuer Versuch!
25 Lächerlich machen wir uns — nimm mir's nicht übel!" —
 „Was sagst du?
Lächerlich?" — „Hättest du nur heut die Dekanin ge-
 hört!
Und in jeglichem Wort ihn selber vernahm ich, den Spötter;
 Boshaft ist er, dazu Schwager zum Pädagogarch."—

„Nun?" — „Einer Festung verglich sie das Haus des Prä-
zeptors, ein Bollwerk
30   Hieß mein Erker, es sei alles bespickt mit Geschütz!" —
„Schnödes Gerede, der lautere Neid! Ich hoffe, mein
Stecken-
Pferd zu behaupten, so gut als ihr Gemahl, der Dekan.
Freut's ihn, Kanarienvögel und Einwerfkäfige dutzend-
Weise zu haben, mich freut's, tüchtigen Essig zu
ziehn." —

Pause. Er scheint nachdenklich. Sie spricht für sich:
35   „Wahrlich, er dauert mich schon: ihn ängstet ein wenig die
Drohung
Mit dem Studienrat, dem er schon lange nicht traut." —

Er fährt fort:

„Als Präzeptor tat ich von je meine Pflicht; ein geschätzter
Gradus neuerlich gibt einiges Zeugnis davon.
Was ich auf materiellem Gebiet, in müßigen Stunden,
40   Manchem Gewerbe, dem Staat denke zu leisten
dereinst,
Ob ich meiner Familie nicht ansehnlichen Vorteil
Sichere noch mit der Zeit, dessen geschweig' ich vor-
erst:
Aber — *den* will ich sehn, der einem geschundenen Schul-
mann
Ein Vergnügen wie das, Essig zu machen, verbeut!
45 Der von Allotrien spricht, von Lächerlichkeiten — er sei nun
Oberinspektor, er sei Rektor und Pädagogarch!
Greife nur einer mich an, ich will ihm dienen! Gewappnet
Findet ihr mich! Dreifach liegt mir das Erz um die
Brust!
— Rike, du lachst! . . . du verbirgst es umsonst! ich fühle die
Stöße . . .
50   Nun, was wandelt dich an? Närrst du mich, törichtes
Weib?" —
„Lieber, närrischer, goldener Mann! wer bliebe hier ernst-
haft?
Nein, dies Feuer hätt' ich nimmer im Essig gesucht!" —
„G'nug mit den Possen! Ich sage dir, mir ist die Sache
nicht spaßhaft." —

„Ruhig! Unseren Streit, Alter, vergleichen wir schon.

55 Gar nicht fällt es mir ein, dir die einzige Freude zu rauben;
        Zuviel hänget daran, und ich verstehe dich ganz.
    Siehst du von deinem Katheder im Schulhaus so durch das
            Fenster
        Über das Höfchen den Schatz deiner Gefäße dir an,
    Alle vom Mittagsstrahl der herrlichen Sonne beschienen,
60   Die, dir den gärenden Wein heimlich zu zeitigen, glüht,
    Nun, es erquicket dir Herz und Aug' in sparsamen Pausen,
        Wie das bunteste Brett meiner Levkoi'n es nicht tat;
    Und ein Pfeifchen Tabak in diesem gemütlichen Anblick
        Nimmt dir des Amtes Verdruß reiner als alles hinweg;
65 Ja, seitdem du schon selbst mit eigenem Essig die rote
        Dinte dir kochst, die sonst manchen Dreibätzner ver-
            schlang,
    Ist dir, mein' ich, der Wust der Exerzitienhefte
        Minder verhaßt; dich labt still der bekannte Geruch.
    Dies, wie mißgönnt' ich es dir? Nur gehst du ein bißchen
            ins Weite.
70   Alles — so heißt dein Spruch — habe sein Maß und
            sein Ziel." —
    „Laß mich! Wenn mein Produkt dich einst zur vermög-
            lichen Frau macht" —
    „Bester, das sagtest du just auch bei der Seidenkultur." —
    „Kann ich dafür, daß das Futter mißriet, daß die Tiere
            krepierten?" —
    „Seine Gefahr hat auch sicher das neue Geschäft." —
75 „Namen und Ehre des Manns, die bringst du wohl gar nicht
            in Anschlag?" —
    „Ehre genug blieb uns, ehe wir Essig gebraut." —
    „Korrespondierendes Mitglied heiß' ich dreier Vereine." —
    „Nähme nur *einer* im Jahr etliche Krüge dir ab!" —
    „Dir fehlt jeder Begriff von rationellem Bestreben." —
80   „Seit du ihn hast, fehlt dir abends ein guter Salat." —
    „Undank! mein Fabrikat durch sämtliche Sorten ist tref-
            flich." —
    „Numero 7 und 9 kenn' ich und — lobe sie nicht." —
    „Heut, wie ich merke, gefällst du dir sehr, mir in Versen zu
            trumpfen." —
        „Waren es Verse denn nicht, was du gesprochen
            bisher?" —

85 „Eine Schwäche des Mannes vom Fach, darfst du sie miß-
brauchen?" —

„Unwillkürlich, wie du, red' ich elegisches Maß." —

„Mühsam übt' ich dir's ein, harmlose Gespräche zu wür-
zen." —

„Freilich im bitteren Ernst nimmt es sich wunderlich
aus." —

„Also verbitt' ich es jetzt; sprich, wie dir der Schnabel ge-
wachsen." —

90 „Gut! laß sehen, wie sich Prose mit Distichen mischt." —

„Unsinn! Brechen wir ab. Mit Weibern sich streiten ist
fruchtlos." —

„Fruchtlos nenn' ich, im Schlot Essig bereiten, mein
Schatz." —

„Daß noch zum Schlusse mir dein Pentameter tritt auf die
Ferse!" —

„Dein Hexameter zieht unwiderstehlich ihn nach." —

95 „Ei, dir scheint er bequem, nur das Wort noch, das letzte, zu
haben:

Hab's! Ich schwöre, von mir hast du das letzte ge-
hört." —

„Meinetwegen, so mag ein Hexameter einmal allein stehn!"

*Pause. Der Mann wir unruhig, es peinigt ihn offenbar, das
Distichon nicht geschlossen zu hören oder es nicht selber
schließen zu dürfen.` Nach einiger Zeit kommt ihm die Frau
mit Lachen zu Hülfe und sagt:*

„Alter, ich tat dir zu viel; wirklich, dein Essig passiert;
Wenn er dir künftig noch besser gerät, wohlan, so ist einzig

100 Dein das Verdienst; denn du hast, wahrlich, kein
zänkisches Weib!" —

Er, gleichfalls herzlich lachend und sie küssend:

„Rike! morgenden Tags räum' ich dir die vorderen Fenster
Sämtlich! und im Kamin prangen die Schinken allein!"

62. ZITRONENFALTER IM APRIL

Grausame Frühlingssonne,
Du weckst mich vor der Zeit,
Dem nur in Maienwonne

Die zarte Kost gedeiht!
5 Ist nicht ein liebes Mädchen hier,
Das auf der Rosenlippe mir
Ein Tröpfchen Honig beut,
So muß ich jämmerlich vergehn,
Und wird der Mai mich nimmer sehn
10 In meinem gelben Kleid.

63. DENK' ES, O SEELE!

Ein Tännlein grünet wo,
Wer weiß, im Walde,
Ein Rosenstrauch, wer sagt,
In welchem Garten?
5 Sie sind erlesen schon,
Denk' es, o Seele!
Auf deinem Grab zu wurzeln
Und zu wachsen.

Zwei schwarze Rößlein weiden
10 Auf der Wiese,
Sie kehren heim zur Stadt
In muntern Sprüngen.
Sie werden schrittweis gehn
Mit deiner Leiche;
15 Vielleicht, vielleicht noch eh'
An ihren Hufen
Das Eisen los wird,
Das ich blitzen sehe!

64. BESUCH IN DER KARTAUSE

Epistel an Paul Heyse

Als Junggesell', du weißt ja, lag ich lang' einmal
In jenem luftigen Dörflein an der Kindelsteig
Gesundheitshalber müßig auf der Bärenhaut.
Der dicke Förster, stets auf mein Pläsier bedacht,
5 Wies mir die Gegend kreuz und quer und führte mich
Bei den Kartäusern gleich die ersten Tage ein.
Nun hätt' ich dir von Seiner Dignität zunächst,
Dem Prior, manches zu erzählen: wie wir uns

In Scherz und Ernst, trotz meines schwäbischen Ketzertums,
10 Gar bald verstanden; von dem kleinen Gartenhaus,
Wo ein bescheidenes Bücherbrett die Lieblinge
Des würdigen Herrn, die edlen alten Schwarten, trug,
Aus denen uns bei einem Glase Wein, wie oft!
Pränestes Haine, Tiburs Wasser zugerauscht.
15 Hievon jedoch ein andermal. Er schläft nun auch
In seiner Ecke dort im Chor. Die Mönche sind,
Ein kleiner Rest der Brüderschaft, in die Welt zerstreut;
Im Kreuzgang lärmt der Küfer, aus der Kirche dampft
Das Malz, den Garten aber deckt ein Hopfenwald,
20 Kaum daß das Häuschen in der Mitte frei noch blieb,
Von dessen Dach, verwittert und entfärbt, der Storch
Auf *einem* Beine traurig in die Ranken schaut.

So, als ich jüngst, nach vierzehn Jahren, wiederkam,
Fand ich die ganze Herrlichkeit dahin. Sei's drum!
25 Ein jedes Ding währt seine Zeit. Der alte Herr
Sah alles lang' so kommen, und ganz andres noch,
Darüber er sich eben nicht zu Tod gegrämt.

Bei dünnem Weißbier und versalzenem Pökelfleisch
Saß ich im Gasthaus, der gewes'nen Prälatur,
30 Im gleichen Sälchen, wo ich jenes erste Mal
Mit andern Fremden mich am ausgesuchten Tisch
Des Priors freute klösterlicher Gastfreiheit.
Ein großer Aal ward aufgetragen, Laberdan
Und Artischocken aus dem Treibhaus; „fleischiger",
35 So schwur, die Lippen häufig wischend, ein Kaplan,
„Sieht sie Fürst Taxis selber auf der Tafel nicht!"
Des höchsten Preises würdig aber deuchte mir
Ein gelber, weihrauchblumiger Vierunddreißiger,
Den sich das Kloster auf der sonnigsten Halde zog.
40 Nach dem Kaffee schloß unser wohlgelaunter Wirt
Sein Raritätenkästchen auf, Bildschnitzerei'n
Enthaltend, alte Münzen, Gemmen und so fort,
Geweihtes und Profanes ohne Unterschied;
Ein heiliger Sebastian in Elfenbein,
45 Desgleichen Sankt Laurentius mit seinem Rost
Verschmähten nicht als Nachbarin Andromeda,
Nackt an den Fels geschmiedet, trefflich schön in Buchs.
Nächst alle dem zog eine altertümliche

Stutzuhr, die oben auf dem Schranke ging, mich an;
50 Das Zifferblatt von grauem Zinn, vor welchem sich
Das Pendelchen nur in allzu peinlicher Eile schwang,
Und bei den Ziffern, groß genug, in schwarzer Schrift
Las man das Wort: *Una ex illis ultima*:
„Derselben eine ist die letzt' " — verdeutschte flugs
55 Der Pater Schaffner, der bei Tisch mich unterhielt
Und gern von seinem Schulsack einen Zipfel wies;
Ein Mann wie Stahl und Eisen; die Gelehrsamkeit
Schien ihn nicht schwer zu drücken, und der Küraß stand
Ihm ohne Zweifel besser als die Kutte an.

60 Dem dacht' ich nun so nach für mich, da streift mein Aug'
Von ungefähr die Wand entlang und stutzt mit eins:
Denn dort, was seh' ich? wäre das die alte Uhr?
Wahrhaftig ja, sie war es! — und vergnügt wie sonst,
Laufst nicht, so gilt's nicht, schwang ihr Scheibchen sich
                                    auf und ab.

65 Betrachtend stand ich eine Weile still vor ihr
Und seufzte wohl dazwischen leichthin einmal auf.
Darüber plötzlich wandte sich ein stummer Gast,
Der einzige, der außer mir im Zimmer war,
Ein älterer Herr, mit freundlichem Gesicht zu mir:
70 „Wir sollten uns fast kennen, mein' ich — hätten wir
Nicht schon vorlängst in diesen Wänden uns gesehn?"
Und alsbald auch erkannt' ich ihn: der Doktor war's
Vom Nachbarstädtchen und weiland der Klosterarzt,
Ein Erzschelm damals, wie ich mich noch wohl entsann,
75 Vor dessen derben Neckerei'n die Mönche sich
Mehr als vor seinem schlimmsten Tranke fürchteten.
Nun hatt' ich hundert Fragen an den Mann und kam
Beiher auch auf das Ührchen. „Ei, jawohl, das ist",
Erwidert' er, „vom seligen Herrn ein Erbstück noch,
80 Im Testament dem Pater Schaffner zugeteilt,
Der es zuletzt dem Brauer, seinem Wirt, vermacht."
— „So starb der Pater hier am Ort?" — „Es litt ihn nicht
Auswärts; ein Jahr, da stellte sich unser Enaksohn,
Unkenntlich fast in Rock und Stiefeln, wieder ein:
85 ‚Hier bleib' ich', rief er, ‚bis man mich mit Prügeln jagt!'
Für Geld und gute Worte gab man ihm denn auch

Ein Zimmer auf der Sommerseite, Hausmannskost
Und einen Streifen Gartenland. An Beschäftigung
Fehlt' es ihm nicht; er brannte seinen Kartäusergeist
90 Wie ehedem, die vielbeliebte Panacee,
Die sonst dem Kloster manches Tausend eingebracht.
Am Abend, wo es unten schwarz mit Bauern sitzt,
Behagt' er sich beim Deckelglas, die Dose und
Das blaue Sacktuch neben sich, im Dunst und Schwul
95 Der Zechgesellschaft, plauderte, las die Zeitung vor,
Sprach Politik und Landwirtschaft — mit *einem* Wort,
Es war ihm wohl, wie in den schönsten Tagen kaum.
Man sagt, er sei bisweilen mit verwegenen
Heiratsgedanken umgegangen — es war damals
100 So ein lachendes Pumpelchen hier, für den Stalldienst, wie
        mir deucht —
Doch das sind Possen. Eines Morgens rief man mich
In Eile zum Herrn Pater: er sei schwer erkrankt.
Ein Schläglein hatte höflich bei ihm angeklopft
Und ihn in größern Schrecken als Gefahr gesetzt.
105 Auch fand ich ihn am fünften oder sechsten Tag
Schon wieder auf den Strümpfen und getrosten Muts.
Doch fiel mir auf, die kleine Stutzuhr, welche sonst
Dem Bette gegenüber stand und allezeit
Sehr viel bei ihm gegolten, nirgend mehr zu sehn.
110 Verlegen, als ich darnach frage, fackelt' er:
Sie sei kaputt gegangen, leider, so und so.
Der Fuchs! dacht' ich, in seinem Kasten hat er sie
Zuunterst, völlig wohlbehalten, eingesperrt,
Wenn er ihr nicht den Garaus etwa selbst gemacht.
115 Das unliebsame Sprüchelchen! Mein Pater fand,
Die alte Hexe fange nachgerade an
Zu sticheln, und das war verdrießlich." — „Exzellent!
Doch setzten Sie den armen Narren hoffentlich
Nicht noch auf Kohlen durch ein grausames Verhör?"
120 — „Je nun, ein wenig stak er allerdings am Spieß,
Was er mir auch im Leben, glaub' ich, nicht vergab."
— „So hielt er sich noch eine Zeit?" — „Gesund und rot
Wie eine Rose sah man Seine Reverenz
Vier Jahre noch und drüber, da denn endlich doch
125 Das leidige Stündlein ganz unangemeldet kam.
Wenn Sie im Tal die Straße gehn dem Flecken zu,
Liegt rechts ein kleiner Kirchhof, wo der Edle ruht.

Ein weißer Stein, mit seinem Klosternamen nur,
Spricht Sie bescheiden um ein Vaterunser an.
130 Das Ührchen aber — um zum Schlusse kurz zu sein —
War rein verschwunden. Wie das kam, begriff kein Mensch.
Doch frug ihm weiter niemand nach, und längst war es
Vergessen, als von ungefähr die Wirtin einst
In einer abgelegenen Kammer hinterm Schlot
135 Eine alte Schachtel, wohl verschnürt und zehenfach
Versiegelt, fand, aus der man den gefährlichen
Zeitweisel an das Tageslicht zog mit Eklat.
Die Zuschrift aber lautete: ,Meinem werten Freund
Bräumeister Ignaz Raußenberger auf Kartaus'."

140 Also erzählte mir der Schalk mit innigem
Vergnügen, und wer hätte nicht mit ihm gelacht?

65. SCHLAFENDES JESUSKIND

gemalt von Franc. Albani

Sohn der Jungfrau, Himmelskind! am Boden
Auf dem Holz der Schmerzen eingeschlafen,
Das der fromme Meister, sinnvoll spielend,
Deinen leichten Träumen unterlegte;
5 Blume du, noch in der Knospe dämmernd
Eingehüllt die Herrlichkeit des Vaters!
O wer sehen könnte, welche Bilder
Hinter dieser Stirne, diesen schwarzen
Wimpern sich in sanftem Wechsel malen!

66. ERINNA AN SAPPHO

(Erinna, eine hochgepriesene junge Dichterin des griechischen Altertums,
um 600 v. Chr., Freundin und Schülerin Sapphos zu Mytilene auf Lesbos.
Sie starb als Mädchen mit neunzehn Jahren. Ihr berühmtestes Werk war ein
episches Gedicht, ,,Die Spindel", von dem man doch nichts Näheres weiß.
Überhaupt haben sich von ihren Poesien nur einige Bruchstücke von wenigen
Zeilen und drei Epigramme erhalten. Es wurden ihr zwei Statuen errichtet,
und die Anthologie hat mehrere Epigramme zu ihrem Ruhme von verschie-
denen Verfassern.)

,,Vielfach sind zum Hades die Pfade", heißt ein
Altes Liedchen — ,,und einen gehst du selber,
Zweifle nicht!" Wer, süßeste Sappho, zweifelt?

Sagt es nicht jeglicher Tag?
5 Doch den Lebenden haftet nur leicht im Busen
Solch ein Wort, und dem Meer anwohnend ein Fischer von
    Kind auf
Hört im stumpferen Ohr der Wogen Geräusch nicht mehr.
— Wundersam aber erschrak mir heute das Herz. Vernimm!

Sonniger Morgenglanz im Garten,
10 Ergossen um der Bäume Wipfel,
Lockte die Langschläferin (denn so schaltest du jüngst
    Erinna!)
Früh vom schwüligen Lager hinweg.
Stille war mein Gemüt; in den Adern aber
Unstet klopfte das Blut bei der Wangen Blässe.

15 Als ich am Putztisch jetzo die Flechten löste,
Dann mit nardeduftendem Kamm vor der Stirn den Haar-
Schleier teilte, — seltsam betraf mich im Spiegel Blick in
    Blick.
Augen, sagt' ich, ihr Augen, was wollt ihr?
Du, mein Geist, heute noch sicher behaust da drinne,
20 Lebendigen Sinnen traulich vermählt,
Wie mit fremdendem Ernst, lächelt halb, ein Dämon,
Nickst du mich an, Tod weissagend!
— Ha, da mit eins durchzuckt' es mich
Wie Wetterschein! wie wenn schwarzgefiedert ein tödlicher
    Pfeil
25 Streifte die Schläfe hart vorbei,
Daß ich, die Hände gedeckt aufs Antlitz, lange
ϳtaunend blieb, in die nachtschaurige Kluft schwindelnd
    hinab.

Und das eigene Todesgeschick erwog ich;
Trockenen Aug's noch erst,
30 Bis da ich dein, o Sappho, dachte
Und der Freundinnen all
Und anmutiger Musenkunst,
Gleich da quollen die Tränen mir.

Und dort blinkte vom Tisch das schöne Kopfnetz, dein Ge-
schenk,

35 Köstliches Byssosgeweb', von goldnen Bienlein schwärmend.
Dieses, wenn wir demnächst das blumige Fest
Feiern der herrlichen Tochter Demeters,
Möcht' ich *ihr* weihn, für meinen Teil und deinen;
Daß sie hold uns bleibe (denn viel vermag sie),
40 Daß du zu früh dir nicht die braune Locke mögest
Für Erinna vom lieben Haupte trennen.

NOTES

1. DER FEUERREITER

The first version of the poem, written in Tübingen in the summer of 1824, comprised only 4 stanzas with the title 'Romanze vom wahnsinnigen Feuerreiter'. In this form it appears in *Maler Nolten*; see Baumann, II, pp. 36 f. In a gathering at which ghost stories are being told, Christoph relates how a pale-faced young man wearing a red cap is seen at a certain window whenever a fire is about to break out. Soon afterwards he gallops out on a bony horse towards the scene of the conflagration. A member of Christoph's audience interrupts him to ask for the version in song, since, he says, the tale 'laut't ja viel besser so und hat gar eine schöne, schauerliche Weise'.

In 1841 Mörike revised the poem, making some stylistic changes and adding what is here stanza 3, in order to make the whole comprehensible without a note on 'wahnsinnig' in the title (Renz, p. 157). In the first version 'der Feuerreiter' is a creature—of either human or supernatural origin—driven by the fascination of fire to daemonic self-sacrifice; in the revised version he is guilty of blasphemy in trying to combat the fire 'mit des heil'gen Kreuzes Span' and his horrible end is a punishment. Woodtli-Löffler and Trümpler (pp. 44 ff.) have shown how young Mörike was dominated by the daemonic aspects of life; after 1832 this characteristic disappeared and references to supernatural forces (e.g. 'die Windesbraut' mentioned in the first version of 'Der Feuerreiter') were removed. The belief in a method of extinguishing fires by magic has long been prevalent among rural communities; the magician is supposed to gallop on a horse round the conflagration three times and then towards water nearby; the flames, following him into the water, are extinguished, but, if the flames reach him before he arrives at the water, he dies. The idea of the red cap bobbing up and down is said to have been inspired in Mörike by the sight of the mad poet Hölderlin pacing up and down his room in a white cap. A student club to which Hauff belonged in Tübingen was called 'Die Feuerreuter'. It is also perhaps significant that in 1824 there was a big fire at the Tübingen 'Klinikum' and that, as a result, a fire brigade was formed. Mörike gives no clear impression of the rider himself, but concentrates on his movement in the first two verses; in contrast the sense of rest in death of the last stanza is partly foreshadowed in the hopeless contest of the rider in the third stanza. The fourth stanza ends the scene of the fire (which is never described in detail), the last bids farewell to the 'Feuerreiter'. See Maync (1), pp. 419–20, v. Wiese (1), pp. 120–1, Zemp. pp. 89–114, Proelß, Mundhenk.

l. 3. **Nicht geheuer:** eery.

l. 7. **gellt:** screams.

l. 11. **sprengt:** gallops at full speed.

l. 15. **Querfeldein!:** across the fields.

l. 21. **den roten Hahn:** fire, cf. 'den roten Hahn aufs Dach setzen.'

l. 24. **besprochen:** charmed away.

l. 42. **Mützen:** archaic weak fem. sing. dat. as in M.H.G.

2. PEREGRINA

Although this cycle has received much attention from scholars and critics, the final meaning, source of inspiration, and even the dating of individual poems are all aspects on which there is no agreement. For the original of Peregrina, see Karl Fischer (2), Corrodi, pp. 47–102, also Reinhardt and Oppel. In the spring of 1823 Mörike had met in Ludwigsburg the wandering servant girl, Maria Meyer of Schaffhausen, with whom, it would seem, he fell passionately in love. She made him unhappy because of her wild, roving way of life and infidelity, yet at one time he regarded her almost as a saint. Eventually he ended this association which meant so much to him, endowing his individual emotions (for which Maria Meyer was not the only source of inspiration) with universal significance in this cycle. The poems were probably written at different times, and first appeared as a group (without **IV**) in *Maler Nolten* (Baumann, II, pp. 350–3). The interpretation of the poems by Kunisch is of particular value to the student. For the relationship of the poems to the novel and the question of dating, see Emmel and Beck (1) (attempts to correct Emmel). Emmel considers that the origins of the theme go back to 1824, but that the first four poems were actually written in the years 1829–30, **V** being the oldest (1827–9); Beck offers more convincing arguments for his view that **II** and **III** were composed about July 1824 and the others in the first half of 1828—he regards **V** as 'entstehungsgeschichtlich den Angelpunkt des Zyklus'.

I. Baumann, I, p. 120, gives an earlier version which has 'Agnes, die Nonne' as the title, 'Weg, reuebringend Liebes-Glück in Sünden!' as l. 8, and the following additional verse, a further expression of the poet's longing to penetrate to the source of life:

> Einst ließ ein Traum von wunderbarem Leben
> Mich sprießend Gold in tiefer Erde seh'n,
> Geheime Lebens-kräfte, die da weben
> In dunkeln Schachten, ahnungsvoll verstehn;
> Mich drang's hinab, nicht konnt' ich widerstreben,
> Und unten, wie verzweifelt, blieb ich stehn, —
> Die goldnen Adern konnt' ich nirgend schauen,
> Und um mich schüttert sehnsuchtsvolles Grauen.

The version in *Maler Nolten* has 'unschuldig Kind' (l. 6), later changed back to 'unwissend Kind', and l. 8 of our text, while the additional verse was already omitted and the title was 'Warnung'.

II. Baumann, I, p. 121, gives the variant of an earlier version (instead of ll. 25–44):

> Wo die Bäume vom Nachttau troffen.
> Und nun strich sie mir, stille stehend,
> Seltsamen Blicks mit dem Finger die Schläfe,
> Jählings versank ich in tiefen Schlummer,
> Aber gestärkt vom Wunderschlafe
> Bin ich erwacht zu glückseligen Tagen,
> Führte die seltsame Braut in mein Haus ein.

This had the title 'Agnesens Hochzeit', while the version in *Maler Nolten*, which is only slightly different, received the title 'Die Hochzeit' with the footnote 'Im Munde des Bräutigams gedacht'.

III. Leffson (IV, p. 227) quotes an early version dated July 6, 1824 (copy in Hartlaub's hand) first published by Karl Fischer and given with slight variation by Krauß (2):

Ein Irrsal kam in die Zaubergärten
Einer fast heiligen Liebe,
Und mit weinendem Blick
Hieß ich das zauberhafte, schlanke
Mädchen
Fern von mir gehen.
Und ihre weiße Stirn,
Drin ein schöner sündhafter Wahnsinn
Aus dem dunklen Auge blickte,
War gesenkt, denn sie liebte mich:
Aber sie zog mit Schweigen
Fort in die graue,
Stille Welt hinaus.

Von der Zeit an
Kamen mir Träume voll schöner Trübe
Wie gesponnen auf Silbergrund,
Wußte nimmer, wie mir geschah —
Und war seliger, leidender Krankheit voll.
Oft in den Träumen zog sich ein Vorhang
Finster und groß ins Unendliche
Zwischen mich und die dunkle Welt,
Hinter ihm ahnt' eine Heide ich,
Hinter ihm hört' ich's mit einemmal
Halb verhalten wie Nachtwind sausen;
Auch die Falten des Vorhangs
Fingen bald im Sturm an sich zu regen,
Gleich einer Ahnung strich es dahinter,
Ruhig blieb ich und bange doch,
Immer leiser wurde der Heidesturm.
Sieh, da kam's!
Aus einer Spalte des Vorhangs
Zuckte [Krauß: 'guckte'] plötzlich der Kopf des Zaubermädchens;
Lieblich war es und doch so beängstigend;
Soll ich die Hand ihr geben
In ihre weiße Hand,
Bittet ihr Auge nicht,
Sagend: Da bin ich wieder
Hergekommen aus weiter Welt?

Baumann, I, p. 121, gives another early version with small variants and the title 'Abschied von Agnes', while the version in *Maler Nolten* is similar except for a few changes in adjectives, l. 18 ('War nur schmachtend, seliger Krankheit voll') and the title ('Scheiden von Ihr').

IV. The differences between Baumann's early version (I, p. 122, title 'Nachklang von Agnes') and our text are unimportant.

V. Early version appears in collection of poems presented to the wife of Mörike's cousin at Buchau on June 19, 1828 (Baumann, I, *Ein Liederheft*, pp. 18–19) with 'verlassen' instead of 'zerrüttet' (l..2) and title 'Verzweifelte

Liebe'. The version in *Maler Nolten* has minor variants and the title 'Und Wieder' (after **IV** 'Scheiden von Ihr'). The poem is close in theme (love) and form (sonnet) to others written in 1828, especially those inspired by the schoolmaster's daughter at Scheer (see Beck).

In *Maler Nolten* Nolten is looking through poems written by his dead friend Larkens and finds 'eine unschuldige Phantasie' concerning his own earlier love for the gipsy Elizabeth. **II** is accompanied by a note referring to a sketch which Nolten made, portraying Elizabeth in Asiatic costume with scenery in a similar style.

Peregrina: Beck notes that the title probably derives from Kerner's *Reiseschatten* (*Sämtliche poetische Werke* III, p. 266, ed. Gaismaier, Leipzig, n.d.) where a girl with magnetic powers (cf. Baumann's variant of **II** above) appears under the name of 'das fremde Mädchen'; the meaning here is 'homeless pilgrim'. Note the parallels with Christ and Mignon, and Mörike's liking for the 'Wanderer' *motif* ('Erbauliche Betrachtung' and 'Fußreise').

I. l. 3. **er** = **der Widerschein.**

l. 7. **kecklich:** boldly.

II. l. 2. **laulicher:** mild.

l. 6. **verschlungenen:** intertwined, interlaced.

ll. 7–8. **das . . . Leicht gegitterte Dach:** delicately latticed roof (of the pavilion, 'Gartengezelte' l. 3).

l. 15. **Mich an der rechten Hand:** holding me by the right hand.

l. 16. **Schwarz gekleidet:** brides wear black in Swabia. **einfach:** in her simplicity.

l. 18. **zierlichen:** neat, dainty.

l. 19. **geht . . . dahin:** goes along. **duftet:** wafts its fragrance.

l. 21. **seitwärts:** aside.

ll. 23–4. **Rosen . . . Lilien:** associated by virtue of their usual colours, red and white, with passion and innocence respectively.

l. 25. **Weymouthsfichte:** North American white pine. That Mörike did not know the tree from personal observation but was attracted by the sound of the word (suggestion of 'Wehmut'), can be seen from his letter to Luise Walther concerning the remark of a forester who admired his poetry (Seebaß (2), 7/8/1874, p. 485). 'Die Stelle mit der Weymouthsfichte soll abgeändert werden. Kiefer statt Fichte ginge ganz wohl an. Ich hatte aber, wie ich jetzt erst finde, überhaupt keine richtige Vorstellung von dem genannten Baum. . . . Die Trauerweide mit ihren hängenden Zweigen wäre offenbar hier weit eher am Platz'.

l. 26. **verhängt:** veils, shrouds.

l. 29. **unteilnehmend:** indifferent.   Nature unsympathetic to Man's problems: cf. 'Besuch in Urach' l. 45.

l. 37. **Spielender Weise:** playfully.

ll. 38ff. The eyelashes twitch like butterflies' wings, until they settle in sleep.

III. l. 1. **Irrsal:** vagary, disturbance, trouble.

l. 17. **ängstig:** troublesome, disquieting.

IV. l. 4. **die Brust in alle Weite dehnen:** extend (stretch) my heart into the far distance. A romantic image.

l. 8. **Bildnis mitleid-schöner Qual:** image of torment made beautiful through pity.

V. l. 4. **sie** = **die Liebe.**

l. 10. **reizender:** more seductive.

l. 11. **in diese Arme dich zu fassen!** let me embrace thee in these arms!

3. AN EINEM WINTERMORGEN, VOR SONNENAUFGANG

This poem was written early in 1825, and was selected by Kurz to open the first edition of the poems. After various unhappy experiences in 1823–4 (Mörike's break with Klärchen Neuffer, Wilhelm Waiblinger and Maria Meyer, the death of his brother August) an uncreative pause ensued. The poet initiated another great creative period with this poem which Beck describes as a 'Genesungsgedicht'. Maync (1) 1, p. 411, shows parallels with 'Morgengemälde' (by the earlier Swabian poet Chr. Ludw. Neuffer whose work Mörike read in Urach) and with the description of the sunrise in Goethe's 'Zueignung' (1784). Sandomirsky, pp. 4–6, regards the poem as romantic, v. Wiese (1), pp. 40–44, is concerned with the conception of time, J. Müller (2) gives a line by line analysis, while Meyer, pp. 39–41 and Beck (1) consider an earlier version in relation to our text. As Meyer asserts, the changes introduced show Mörike's efforts to heighten pregnancy of expression, avoid vagueness and increase the vividness of the imagery. J. Müller sees 'eine erstaunliche Goethenähe' in the work. The poem is also examined in detail by Margaret Mare, pp. 30–2, and Kohlschmidt.

An iambic metre of 5 beats to a line is used with occasional variation through a dactyl at the beginning of the line (ll. 5, 13, 26, 30, 31; cf. 'Auf eine Christblume'). The poem has 6 sections, all with their own rhyming systems and most of them differing in length; (1) 4 lines a b b a (2) 6 lines a b a b c c (3) 7 lines a b b a c c b (4) 5 lines a b a a b (5) 11 lines a b b a c d c c d e e (6) 6 lines a a b c b c.

(1) The poet addresses early morning in winter, welcoming that time of transition which has often inspired him to poetic vision.

(2) His soul seems purified as though in anticipation of the magic powers which are near at hand and which will bring poetic inspiration from the clear blue air (l. 9 'aus dem klaren Gürtel blauer Luft'): l. 7 suggests that the boundaries between the poet himself and the world around him become blurred. This thought is taken up in (3), where he finds it difficult to focus his eyes and his thoughts on reality, as a world of colour and beauty appears to him; the vowels of l. 13 are carefully chosen to suggest through their melody something of the magic of his vision.

In (4), as Beck has pointed out, extensive use is made of umlaut forms, especially 'ä'; here Mörike has visions arising from two sources of inspiration to him, the Christian (a Christmas image associated with winter) and that of classical literature (l. 20). As in the previous section Mörike longs to know by what agency the visions come to him. (5) portrays how the poet's joy and confidence grow as he feels creative intuition, l. 28 ('Der Genius jauchzt in mir!') marking the climax of the poem; he brushes aside the melancholy which is an obstacle to his creative mood and believes that if he grasps the moment given to him now, all his difficulties may be overcome (l. 33 'Es ist ein Augenblick, und alles wird verwehn'!) In (6) the divine power which inspires him is presented to us, as it were, through the glorious moment of sunrise.

Sandomirsky has noted that, except in the last lines, enjambment has not been employed, each line having a unity and ending with punctuation; relatively unimportant words are used to begin the line, the stress of meaning falling later. A remarkable feature of the poem is the use of compound adjective forms created by the poet.

4. GESANG ZU ZWEIEN IN DER NACHT

Written in its first form in 1825, this poem appears in the dramatic frag-
ment *Spillner* (1826–7, Baumann, I, pp. 633 ff.) where the hero, at the window
of the student prison at night, feels 'eine nie gefühlte Frömmigkeit, Inbrunst,
gesund helläugigt Leben' and seems to hear 'das Zittern der Luft, das so
eigen ist, wenn die Nacht die ersten Berührungen des Morgens spürt'.
These emotions lead him to the involuntary creation and recital of the poem.

In *Maler Nolten* (Baumann, II, pp. 109–111) the poem is linked with the
following ('Nachts') both being introduced into the shadow-play 'Der
letzte König von Orplid' (sc. 4), where Ulmon, the king of Orplid, speaks
with the fairy princess Thereile (she loves Ulmon, but he hates her because
she has ensnared him by magic). Ulmon speaks ll. 1–6 of 'Nachts', next
Thereile ll. 1–6 of this poem, then Ulmon ll. 7–10, Thereile ll. 11–17, Ulmon
ll. 18–24: thereafter follow Ulmon's monologue ('Nachts' ll. 7–12) and two
lines: 'In meiner Brust, die kämpft und ruht, / Welch eine Ebbe, welche Flut!'

In *Spillner* the lines had not been split up into dialogue, and were pub-
lished in this earlier form in 1838 with ll. 7–10, 18–24 omitted and the title
'Nachts'. Writing in 1854 to Mörike, Storm expressed preference for the
1838 version rather than the later one (our text) 'denn diesen wunderbaren
Versen, worin der Dichter uns die Urform der Dinge zu offenbaren scheint,
sind die andern Teile des Gedichts nicht ebenbürtig und die ersteren bilden
ohnehin ein geschlossenes Ganze für sich' (Rath, (2), p. 71).

The poem has been examined by Wilhelm Schneider, Grenzmann, and
v. Wiese (1), pp. 64–9, who stresses the contrast between Man and Woman
in the dialogue (a form also employed in 'Aus der Ferne' 1846): 'Der Mann
nimmt die vom Ohr als Klang und Musik erlebte Welt der Frau auf, führt
sie durch das Auge ins männlich Bewußtsein und Abstand Gewinnende
weiter, um dann mit der Antwort der Frau wieder in den Ursprungs-
bereich der Töne, in Gesang und Sphärenklang zurückgeholt zu werden'.

Reinhold, p. 143, finds a parallel in the dialogue at the beginning of the
fifth act of Shakespeare's *Merchant of Venice*.

l. 3 **der freche Tag:** day is audacious (Swabian: see note to l. 3 of 'Jung
Volkers Lied') because it is associated with a human activity which drowns
the natural sounds but cannot detract from their much greater significance.

l. 4. **der Erdenkräfte flüsterndes Gedränge:** the primitive and original
forces which can be heard working at night; a clear link with 'Nachts'.

l. 11. **Wie ein Gewebe zuckt...:** the woman's speech is generally more
poetic and imaginative than the man's.

l. 14. **sel'gen Feen:** blessed (happy) fairies.

l. 15. **Sphärenklang:** the music of the spheres mentioned in *Faust* ('Prolog
im Himmel').

ll. 13–17. Schaeffer (p. 62) comments: 'So wird in einer kindlich reinen
Musik, einem Lautspiel von Vokalen -e-en und i-en in melodischem
Wechsel, von jenen Geheimnissen berichtet, die in Traumgesichten ihres
Schlafs im Gehäus der Natur der Seele offenbar wurden'.

l. 19. An impression of the softness of the landscape, black at night, grow-
ing green with the coming light.

l. 24. Night (which is kindly disposed, l. 18 'holde Nacht') is in a state of
ecstasy, and this mood is shared by the soul of creation, the spirit of life.

The metre is mainly iambic, the basis being a line of 5 beats which is
sometimes varied. Each section has a different rhyming pattern.

5. NACHTS

Written before 1834 (Maync) or 1823 (Ibel), this poem certainly does not belong to the Cleversulzbach period (Maurer's assertion); it is related to 'Gesang zu zweien in der Nacht' in both theme and metre and, since it was never published during Mörike's lifetime, may be regarded as incomplete. In an appendix to his article on 'An einem Wintermorgen . . .' Beck points out the importance of 'Nachts' for the *Weltanschauung* of young Mörike. In 'Der letzte König von Orplid' Ulmon expresses through the lines of the poem longing for love and memory of love (see note on 'Gesang zu zweien in der Nacht' for use of 'Nachts' in the play).

In the 'Widerspiel von Fülle und Entbehrung' Ulmon recalls the forgotten name of his wife, while 'nimmersatt' (l. 9) is used here as an attribute of love (cf. 'Nimmersatte Liebe' and 'Mein Fluß'). Beck shows that this shorter version introduced into the shadow-play (down to 'Entbehrung') acquired a different meaning when the last 6 lines were added; now 'Fülle und Entbehrung' refer not to love but to a paradoxical kind of participation in Nature. 'Entbehrung' suggests that in some ways this participation is inadequate (cf. 'Besuch in Urach'). Beck interprets ll. 13-14 as a desire by the poet to separate himself from Nature and return to the world of Man, his heart not being at home in either sphere ('schwankendes' l. 15), while 'beuge dich' (l. 18) is given the meaning 'Füge dich den Grenzen der Menschheit': this approach, reflecting Mörike's usual attitude to Nature—like Faust he is attracted and yet terrified by natural forces beyond his full comprehension—explains difficulties which are not resolved by v. Wiese in his remarks on the poem ((1) pp. 64-9).

Beck considers that Mörike probably excluded the poem from his published work because he could not express the idea in the verses as clearly as he wished. Brigitte Müller, p. 49, believes that the end of the poem shows the poet eager to free himself from human bonds but unable to do so (this inability seen as a weakness).

In the first section of the poem (ll. 1-6) Mörike concentrates on the activity of Nature at night. The rest of the poem contrasts the abundance of Nature's powers, insatiable and fermenting, with her paradoxical tranquillity and deliberate orderliness ('Wohlbedacht' l. 10), concentrating finally on the poet's own emotions face to face with Nature. The metre has a 5 beat iambic basis, but some divergence from this in scanning is both possible and desirable, especially in ll. 1-2. The rhyming system is (1) a a b c b c, (2) a a b c c b d d e f e f.

6 and 7. JUNG VOLKER and JUNG VOLKERS LIED

In *Maler Nolten* (Baumann, II, pp. 282 ff.) Mörike presents a number of his characters resting at a place, the description of which is partly inspired, according to a footnote, by the author's acquaintance with the landscape near Groß-Bettlingen, in the Nürtingen district. Amandus tells the story of a robber chief Marmetin, known as Jung Volker, who once frequented the area; at the head of his band he plundered the rich, arrogant nobles and gave generously to the poor peasants. 'Voll körperlicher Anmut, tapfer, besonnen, leutselig und doch rätselhaft in allen Stücken, galt er bei seinen Gesellen fast für ein überirdisches Wesen, und sein durchdringender Blick mäßigte ihr Benehmen bis zur Bescheidenheit herunter'. Jung Volker, it is related, was drawn to certain places, especially a hill where he assembled his band and where he often sat alone to make music to the four winds on 'eine alte abgemagerte Geige', facing each direction in turn. Other stories are told which inspire sympathy and interest for a heroic yet enigmatic, even daemonic, character, e.g. his mother (an enchantress) was said to have carried him off while he was on his way to Jerusalem. The narrator recalls some verses about his fabulous birth which make him, 'gar charakteristisch für den freien kräftigen Mann, zu einem Sohne des Windes'. Then 'Jung Volkers Lied' is sung (p. 288, with minor textual differences from our version), to be followed by 'Jung Volker' (pp. 288-9) with variants including:

(a) the introduction of a short line suggesting an echo after l. 4 in each stanza: st. 1, Ja Winde!: st. 2, Ja blitzen!: st. 3, Ja Herde!

(b) more references to the observer who is only mentioned once in our version: st. 3, Ich sah ihn schleudern die Geig' in die Luft, / Ich sah ihn sich werfen zu Pferde; / Da hörten wir alle, wie er ruft: ... Our version emphasizes more strongly the speed of Jung Volker's reactions to danger and the fact that he is defending, not attacking.

In June, 1832, F. Th. Vischer asked Mörike whether he composed the story of Jung Volker 'ohne allen historischen Fingerdeut' (Robert Vischer, p. 84), but it is not known if he received a reply. Mörike had warned readers against looking for his sources (footnote, Baumann, II, p. 286). It seems probable that the figure was invented as the personification of the free man (son of the wind) and as the 'noble robber' (cf. Schiller's Karl Moor). Volker is the name of the famous warrior musician in the *Nibelungenlied*. Mörike made a sketch of Jung Volker in which his instrument resembles a guitar (Krauß (1) p. 121).

JUNG VOLKER

Written 1826.

l. 4. **Nach dem just:** according to ... **just** = gerade.

l. 7. **spielt auf:** plays (for dancing).

l. 11. **Seine blauen Augen ihm blitzen. ihm:** dative as in 'Der (Mein) Arm tut mir weh'. Note alliteration, here and elsewhere in the poem, also repetition and apocope, all features inspired by the *Volkslied*.

l. 17. **Pfeifchen:** possibly his whistle. Hieber (p. 164) sees this as a manifestation of Jung Volker's daemonic relationship to the wind; 'Ein Windstoß ist's, nichts anderes, der sich pfeifend erhebt, der Zweige und Äste bricht und in die Höhe wirbelt'.

JUNG VOLKERS LIED

Exact date of composition unknown; possibly *c.* 1826. Many features of the *Volkslied* may be noted, e.g. use of 'und' in introductory lines, colloquialisms, repetition.

l. 3. **frech:** F. Th. Vischer (p. 38) noted that this word was used in the Swabian sense (= **frei:** 'Ausdruck von Kühnheit und Selbstgefühl').

l. 7. **Des Windes Braut:** cf. Woodtli-Löffler. Jung Volker's supernatural qualities are explained.

8. BESUCH IN URACH

Written in May, 1827. Maync ((1), I, p. 414) points out parallels in Goethe's 'Ilmenau' and the Faust monologue 'Des Lebens Pulse schlagen frisch lebendig' (*Faust* II, ll. 4679-4747), also F. Th. Vischer's poem (dependent on

Mörike's for both motive and style, a reminiscence of years at the seminary) 'Geschrieben in der Felshöhle am Klosterberg in St. . . .]' (*Auch Einer*, III, pp. 383 ff., Stuttgart / Leipzig, 1903). Urach is a small town at the foot of the 'Schwäbische Alb', lying amidst hills and famous locally for its waterfall. Mörike attended the seminary there from October 1818 until 1822. In this poem, written in *ottava rima*, Mörike uses his impressions of a return to the well-known scene, after an absence of about five years, to consider the personal problems of (*a*) communion and relationship with Nature, and (*b*) coming to terms with his former self (for he has lost his childhood and innocence). There is a valuable analysis by v. Wiese (1) pp. 51-3.

In the first stanza, Mörike, struggling with his emotions and the memory of his former self, now alien to him, falls into that sense of vision and unreality reflected in 'An einem Wintermorgen . . .' in which surrounding objects appear almost as though out of focus; this impression is strengthened by carefully selected, often dynamic verb forms (l. 2 'verirrt', l. 4 'schwankt', 'schwirrt', l. 6 'verwirrt'). The impact of the scene on the poet is immediately conveyed. In the second stanza Mörike exhorts this familiar landscape to recognize him, approaching it subjectively; thus the rocks, 'Wolkenstühle' or chairs amidst the clouds—an image to stress their height—, seem erected once more in his sight, 'wieder aufgerichtet', as though they had no real existence of their own. The memories recalled by the scene are both painful and pleasant to the poet (stanza 3), but he brushes them aside ('Hinweg!' l. 25, stanza 4), longing to penetrate into the secrets of Nature, here embodied in the source of the waterfall. Now follows the fifth stanza. Believing at first that Nature may reveal herself by speaking, as it were, aloud to herself of her secrets (perhaps through the sound of running water) the poet then turns from this hope with the thought that she is bound to silence by her own laws and that he must therefore take the initiative in approaching her—thus he offers his bared breast to the pillar of water at the fall, seeking by this almost despairing gesture the intimacy and communion for which he longs (cf. 'Mein Fluß', l. 35, 'Mein Leben um das deine'). Mörike seems to experience this desire for communication with Nature almost as a physical need, yet it cannot be fulfilled for him (stanza 6). Nature remains unfeeling towards him and has always been indifferent to Man's emotions, he reflects.

Leaving the shade of the trees by the waterfall, the poet finds his way to a homely nook which evokes bitter-sweet reminiscence (stanza 7—the little bench and hut had definite counterparts in reality, see Karl Fischer ((1), p. 37). He remembers first a school friend, and then his younger self (stanza 8) whom he longs to meet and understand (stanza 9). Thoughts of his happiness in the past evoke in him exhaustion and pain that pleasure no longer has a place in his life, when the electric atmosphere of an approaching storm refreshes him (stanza 10). The thunder storm (storms are violent and prolonged in Urach because the town is surrounded by hills) is portrayed in stanza 11, and the poet's leave-taking from this dearly loved spot in the last stanza.

l. 4. **Staude:** shrub.

l. 10. **Besonnte:** shone on by the sun, sunny.

l. 11. **wo kaum der Mittag lichtet:** where 'tis scarcely light at midday (because of the density of the forests).

l. 14. **süßschläferndem:** sweetly somnolent.

l. 18. **mich in liebliche Betrachtung fängt:** ensnares me in pleasant reflexion.

l. 19. **so geringe:** of such small account.

l. 40. **ob sie dir sich teile!:** [to test] whether it [the water] will part for thee!

l. 44. Translate: it ('deine Seele') flees, no matter how I long to drown myself in thee!

l. 45. **Dich kränkt's nicht:** Thou carest not.

l. 59. **sonder Harm:** without guile, innocent.

l. 61. *alten* **Sonne:** sun of old times (his schooldays).

l. 81. **finstre Ballen schließen:** mass in gloomy clusters.

l. 83. **den alten Riesen:** thunder.

9. SEPTEMBERMORGEN

Written October 18, 1827; original title 'Herbstfrühe'. The essence of autumn is presented in the suggestion of the eventual victory of the sun over the mist. Anticipation of the event is indicated in 'noch' (l. 1), 'noch' (l. 2), and 'bald' (l. 3).

l. 5. **Herbstkräftig:** a compound invented by Mörike: 'with the vigour of autumn'. **gedämpfte:** dulled (of colour).

10. UM MITTERNACHT

Written in October, 1827, the poem concluded the first edition of Mörike's *Gedichte*: here and in the second edition the first word was 'Bedächtig', later replaced by 'Gelassen'. For valuable comment on this poem, see v. Wiese (1), pp. 69–70, Schütze, pp. 119–20, Ermatinger, II, pp. 214–15, Goes (2), Pfeiffer (1) and (2), Weißer and Staiger (4), pp. 31–2. Lines 1–4 portray the falling of Night over the land and the coming of midnight, when there seems to be a moment of pause as Day and Night have equal weight in the scales of Time. Night, personified, appears as a mother figure in the second half of the stanza—she is mother, too, to the streams who sing to her of the day that is past. In the second stanza we are told that Night does not listen to the song of the waters, one she has heard many times before and of which she is weary. Its monotony of form and theme is suggested in the phrase 'Das uralt alte Schlummerlied' (l. 9). Her longing is directed away from the song of the day (associated for the poet with human activity, cf.'Gesang zu zweien in der Nacht' l. 3) towards the eternal, symbolized in 'Des Himmels Bläue' (l. 11) and the equipoise of the fleeting hours (l. 12). Yet the streams are not dismayed by her indifference and sing on in their sleep. Night and Day are contrasted, not only in the images of Night and running streams, but also in the polarity of rest and movement such as we find in C. F. Meyer's poem 'Der römische Brunnen'. This polarity is underlined by a skilful manipulation of rhythm: the tranquil, iambic metre of the first four lines in each stanza suggests the dreamy, visionary and static character of Night, while ll. 5–8 and 13–16 have a mixed metre (iambic-anapaestic) conveying the rippling movement and dynamic quality of the water. The last two lines of each stanza constitute a refrain which is intimately linked with the stanza itself. The arrangement of light and dark vowels plays an important part in the total effect, one of melodious beauty. The poem is an example of Mörike's ability to portray lyric emotion in plastic form. Rhymed couplets are employed and the length of the line is varied. l. 11 contains an example of synaesthesia.

11. IM FRÜHLING

Written at Scheer on May 13, 1828, at one sitting in the early morning (Krauß (2), p. 102); in a letter accompanying a copy of the poem to Mährlen, Mörike describes the setting; 'Hier sitz' ich und schreib' ich in dem besonnten Garten des hiesigen katholischen Pfarrers. Die Laube, wo mein Tisch und Schreibzeug steht, läßt durch's junge Geißblatt die Sonne auf mein Papier spielen. Der Garten liegt etwas erhöht; über die niedrige Mauer weg, auf der man sich, wie einem Gesimse, setzen kann, sieht man unmittelbar auf den Wiesenplan, auf welchem die Donau ihre Scheere bildet'.

In *Maler Nolten* (Baumann, II, pp. 251 ff.) Nolten feels 'eine mächtige Sehnsucht . . . ein süßer Drang nach einem namenlosen Gute, das ihn allenthalben aus den rührenden Gestalten der Natur so zärtlich anzulocken und doch wieder in eine unendliche Ferne sich ihm zu entziehen schien'. Mörike now seeks to express these feelings in the poem, which then follows.

From the graphically portrayed setting ('Frühlingshügel') the poet seems carried away into revery as though borne on a passing cloud; he would like to find Love (for him something unique—'alleinzig') and stay with it, but Love, like the winds, is homeless (cf. 'Lied vom Winde'). After a pause there follows a poetic impression of the soul open to a mood of longing; Mörike, although impelled by love and hope, wonders what Spring wants of him and when his longing will be stilled. In the final section his attention is drawn once more to his surroundings, the cloud mentioned earlier, the river and the warmth of the sun which seems to permeate his very being. Drowsy and intoxicated, he sees no more, only hears the sound of the bee. Various thoughts enter his mind and, unsure of the precise goal of his longing, or the nature of the emotion it inspires, he turns for satisfaction to memories of the past.

Mörike's longing, unlike that of the Romantics, finds an end—poetically transfigured (hence 'unnennbare') experiences of the past, perhaps of childhood or of the Orplid fantasies in the Tübingen period. Beauty and subtlety of rhythm are achieved by variations in the length of the line and in the metre; the rhyming system differs in each section, (1) a a b c c b, (2) a b b a c c, (3) a a b c b c d d e e f f e. Jacob (p. 44) sums up the poem well as 'eine tiefgreifende Verwandlung seelischer Art, bei der Seele, Körper und Natur untrennbar beteiligt sind'.

12. FRAGE UND ANTWORT

Written 1828. See note to 'Nimmersatte Liebe'.

Two questions are asked in the first stanza, (1) How does Love, which causes the poet disquiet, come to his heart? (2) Why has he allowed it to torment him for so long? These questions are parried rather than answered in stanzas 2 and 3 respectively by the introduction of parallels from nature; thus the mysterious workings of inner human experience are compared with unfathomable and uncontrollable natural phenomena. Cf. 'Lied vom Winde'.

13. NIMMERSATTE LIEBE

In 1828 Mörike stayed for some time with his brother Karl at Scheer on the Danube; this poem, written that same year, was one of a number inspired by his love for the daughter of the local schoolmaster (others include 'Frage und Antwort', 'Josephine' and 'Liebesvorzeichen'). Mörike's sensuality is clearly revealed in the erotic tone. Ermatinger (III, pp. 136-7) has contrasted this poem with Storm's 'Weiße Rosen' (1) which is more restrained in expression (the girl bites her lips in anger at the memory of her faithless lover's kiss). The insatiability of youthful passion is suggested by a striking image ('ein Sieb mit eitel Wasser füllen') and by the girl's passive acceptance and perverse enjoyment of physical pain. Note the use of apocope (**Lieb', Ruh'**) in the style of the *Volkslied*. The three stanzas vary in length and form: (1) 7 lines rhyming a b a b c c b — general observation on theme, (2) 8 lines, a b a b c d c d—personal application, (3) 4 lines, a b a b—reversion to general observation; all are linked by theme and repetition of 'die Lieb' '.

l. 6 **gar**: fully, completely.

l. 18. **Salomo**: Solomon, the great lover by convention; he had 700 wives and 300 concubines according to Kings I, ch. 11, v. 3.

14. AUF DER REISE

Written 1828, possibly in Scheer. The theme (parting from the beloved) and some of the features introduced (post-horn, moonlight, double) are of romantic origin, but the poem springs from real experience. For the mixture of pleasure and pain felt by the poet (ll. 1-2) and the uncertainty of his desires (l. 12) cf. 'Im Frühling'. Variations in metre and length of line suggest the jolting of the coach. The stanzas differ in length and rhyming system, (1) 5 lines a b b a b, (2) 6 lines a b a a b a, (3) 10 lines a a b b c c d e e d, (4) 4 lines a b a b. This treatment of a hackneyed theme shows Mörike's originality and is a fine example of his 'Wanderlieder'.

l. 20. **bescheidentlich**: modestly. For form cf. 'wonniglich' in 'Verborgenheit' l. 12.

15. LIED VOM WINDE

Written 1828; original title 'Die Windsbraut'. The wind has a daemonic power for Mörike, see Woodtli-Löffler and Trümpler (pp. 37 ff., 44 ff.). Hermann Kurz commented in a letter to Mörike, 'Du weißt den Schrecken zu handhaben, wie ein Mädchen ihre Kochlöffel' (Kindermann, p. 167). In *Maler Nolten* (Baumann, II, pp. 384 ff.) Agnes, in her madness, sings 'das Windlied' on top of a wind-swept hill, modulating her voice for question or answer and gesticulating. The speaker asks the wind where its home is to be found (ll. 1-3). The winds (plural) reply: they have sought an answer from the mountains, seas and heavens without success: they rush on, advising her to ask their brother winds (ll. 4-17). The speaker tries to hold them up with another question—where is Love's home, where its beginning and end? (ll. 18-21). They think she is joking ('schelmisches Kind'); who knows? they reply, Love is like wind, never-resting, eternal but inconstant. Ironically they promise to convey a greeting to the beloved as they bid farewell.

The length of the lines is varied and a tripping, mixed metre is employed; there is a complicated rhyming system with an occasional 'orphan'. Repetition ('viel vielen', 'weit weiten') and alliteration ('Rasch' . . . 'Ruhet', 'Wälder und Wiesen') occur. For theme cf. 'Frage und Antwort'.

16. ANTIKE POESIE

Written 1828; other sonnets of this year are 'Eberhard Wächter' and 'Seltsamer Traum'. In this poem Mörike pays homage to Goethe (mentioned as the author of *Iphigenie auf Tauris* l. 11), contrasting the inspiration of his presence with the atmosphere after his influence has waned (l. 14 'frostig rauhe Lüfte'—the tendency, which had already begun, to turn away from poetry to political and social questions in literature. A clear indication of Mörike's preference for literature of the preceding age.

l. 1. **Helikon:** the Boeotian mountain of the ancients sacred to the Muses.

l. 6. **der heil'ge Quell:** the Castalian spring on Parnasuss whose waters were said to bring poetic inspiration.

Iambic 5 beat lines with masculine and feminine rhymes, those with a feminine ending having an extra unstressed syllable: rhyming system a b b a   a b b a   c d c   c d c.

17. MEIN FLUSZ

Written 1828, and probably inspired by the Danube at Scheer. See the perceptive and scholarly analysis by Prawer (1) (pp. 167–74) who indicates three levels at which the poem can be read, experience of (1) swimming, (2) physical love, and (3) life itself. The claims for the interpretation in (2) are strengthened by evidence of other erotic poetry and of poems concerned with the problems of love written about this time, e.g. 'Nimmersatte Liebe', 'Frage und Antwort', 'Liebesvorzeichen' and 'Josephine'. The longing to penetrate into Nature's secrets and the subsequent failure to do so (final stanza) recall 'Besuch in Urach': in his striving to establish an intimate relationship with the element (note **Mein Fluß**) Mörike uses an approach similar to that of Goethe in the first stanza of 'Wechsel'. The poem is remarkable for its 'word music' which is achieved by a subtle arrangement of vowels and consonants, by alliterative devices and by repetition of f, pf, s, ss, sch, w and g in various combinations. The metre, an iambic 4 or 3 beat line (4 3 4 3 4 4 3 in stanza of 7 lines) helps to convey the impression of water ebbing and flowing.

l. 5. I feel it already up to my breast.

l. 6. **Liebesschauerlust:** a romantic compound with oxymoron—'shudder and pleasure of love'.

l. 10. **aus und ein:** to and fro.

ll. 15 ff. Like the wind ('Lied vom Winde') the river is in a hurry and unlikely to divulge those secrets which the poet longs to learn: it does not seem to be fully initiated into such secrets itself and appears, as it struggles to express itself intelligibly, to be intent on asking questions.

l. 22. **kinderrein:** a compound suggesting purity and innocence.

l. 25. **ihn = den Himmel** (the river's soul; the blueness of the sky is reflected in the river).

l. 28. **erschwingen:** attain.

l. 29. **sie = die Bläue.**

l. 32. **Wechselscheine:** change of appearance.

ll. 33 ff. Brigitte Müller, p. 38, regards these lines as among the most moving in Mörike's work; here, she declares, he approaches the river as a lover and is ready to sacrifice his own human existence to attain the union with Nature which he desires—such an offering, inevitably leading to his destruction, can only be regarded as 'Liebestod'. This desperate but ineffectual gesture is certainly the climax of the poem and recalls ll. 39-40 of 'Besuch in Urach' ('Dir biet' ich denn, begier'ge Wassersäule, / Die nackte Brust, ach, ob sie dir sich teile!')

ll. 36 ff. The final stanza marks a return to sober reality. The river, unmoved by his plea, seems to point the way back to the bank and the poet has to resign himself to failure. The result is a mood of acceptance tinged with regret: he thinks of the river as happy in its independence, but then recalls that it is a part of Mother Nature, to which it must return despite its wanderings. The 'ew'ge Mutterquelle' is a source of life which Mörike shares with the river, and this idea, not directly expressed, is possibly a source of consolation to him and would explain the conciliatory note in the last lines of the poem.

18. DIE TRAURIGE KRÖNUNG

Written 1828, possibly at Scheer, this 'Romanze' (as Mörike described it) was sent to Vischer in 1833 in a form which included minor textual changes. Vischer commented (Robert Vischer, pp. 106-7, letter of 22/10/1833): 'Deine Ballade hat große poetische Wirkung auf mich gemacht. Die längeren Endzeilen der Reime, in denen sich von vornherein das tragische Ende zwischen die Erzählung angstvoll hereindrängen will, sind wie ein lang hinzuckender und dann verschwindender Blitz auf dem dunkeln Grunde. Das nickende, trippelnde, freundliche Kind ist ganz Shakespearisch angeschaut und weit schauerlicher als eine quantitativ größere und furchtbarere Erscheinung'. Mörike intended to include the poem in a religious novel on which he was working in 1833 (this remained uncompleted). The story was invented and given a vaguely Irish (i.e. *märchenhaft*) setting. Liffey (l. 6) is the river on which Dublin stands. Maurer (p. 167) has noted the parallel with Banquo's ghost in *Macbeth* and the fact that in both cases the murderer alone sees the spectre. When reviewing the first edition of Mörike's poems, F. Th. Vischer (p. 38) characterized the ballad as 'voll Gewitterschwüle und tragischer Angst, ganz im Geiste des Macbeth'. There are interpretations by Stählin and Rahn.

In the first stanza the situation is described simply with brief comment, as it were, from the chorus in the last line. In the second stanza the king sits confused ('irr'') among the tokens of his new splendour and bids his son bring him the crown once more (so that he may gloat over this symbol of his power). In answer a procession of ghosts ('Totenspiel') approaches softly with the crown in their midst (stanza 3): an eery effect is achieved by the use of the impersonal 'es drängt', while in the fourth stanza 'es' is also employed with this association, grammatically, however, as the pronoun for 'das Kind'. Both the third and the fourth stanzas conclude with a reference to the king, he is 'geisterschwül', oppressed by the presence of spirits and later terrified by the appearance of the dead child's ghost and the offer of a crown from him. He is literally frightened to death, and his fear is intensified by the consciousness of his own guilt. A daemonic power stronger than Man is at work within him. In the final stanza a concise but impressive description of the scene leads to the deep silence indicating the king's death; this conclusion recalls in some respects that of Goethe's 'Erlkönig'. The crown is prominent throughout as a symbol of power, but a distinction is drawn

between the earthly crown for which the king calls (l. 4, l. 13 'die **Krone**')
and the crown brought by the spirits (vaguely presented as 'eine **Krone**',
l. 18, l. 27). The metre is basically iambic; 7 line stanzas are used, rhymed
a b a b c c a with an effective alternation of masculine and feminine rhymes.

l. 3. **meuchelte:** murdered.

l. 5. **Prangen:** display.

l. 6. **begangen:** celebrated ('ein Fest begehen').

l. 24. **sterbensweh:** in mortal pain.

l. 27. **reichet** = **reicht.**

l. 28. **des** = **dessen. Herze** = **Herz.**

l. 29. **strich:** suggests disappearance in silence.

l. 34. **tät sich neigen** = **neigte (neigt) sich.**

l. 35. **neiget** = **neigt.**

19. IN DER FRÜHE

Written in 1828. After a sleepless night of doubt and anxiety, Mörike
rejoices at the approach of dawn. The time of transition from night to day
is often one of inspiration and vision for him, cf. 'An einem Wintermorgen,
vor Sonnenaufgang'. See interpretations by Tschirsch and Stein.

l. 2. **gehet . . . herfür:** appears (archaic, 'hervorgehen').

l. 4. **wühlet:** 'burrows'—the suggestion of gnawing anxiety.

l. 9. **dorten:** archaic form of 'dort' used for rhyme.

20. DIE GEISTER AM MUMMELSEE

Written in 1828. Mummelsee is a lake in the Black Forest. In a slightly
different version the poem appears in *Maler Nolten* (Baumann, II, pp. 124–5)
in scene 9 of the *Schattenspiel* 'Der letzte König von Orplid': the stage direc-
tions are 'Nacht. Mondschein. Waldiges Tal. Mummelsee. Im Hinter-
grunde den Berg herab gegen den See schwebt ein Leichenzug von beweg-
lichen Nebelgestalten. Vorne auf dem Hügel der König, starr nach dem
Zuge blickend. Auf der andern Seite, unten, den König nicht bemerkend,
zwei Feenkinder. Die Feenkinder im Zwiegespräch'. The poem is 'eine
visionäre Vorwegnahme' (Trümpler, p. 77) of King Ulmon's death, with the
scene described in dialogue by the two fairies. After the words of the poem
have been spoken, the stage directions inform us, the fairy children flee,
the king shouts after the procession (moving up the mountain again) and to
his queen Almissa (l. 18 'die glänzende Frau') that the coffin, supposed to
contain his corpse, is empty: later, however, he wonders if he is still alive
after all.

The first stanza poses a question and awakes interest: what is that (pur-
posely left vague and impersonal) descending the mountain with cheerful-
sounding song—can it be people going to a dance or feast? Then the com-
panion corrects this mistaken impression. It is a funeral procession, the
music is their lamentation, and they (later named as the spirits of the lake) are
bringing the royal magician back to the lake (for burial). The atmosphere of
mystery and eeriness, conjured up by the words 'wieder' and 'Die Geister vom
See' in stanza 2, is intensified in stanza 3 by suggestive verbs ('schweben',
'schwirren'), the idea of the spirits entering the water without wetting their
feet, the sudden reference to the wife beside the coffin and the repetition of
'sie'. All this is preparation for the presentation of an even greater wonder,

the opening of the waters to admit the procession, which gradually disappears. In stanzas 4 and 5 attention is concentrated on the surface of the lake. In the last stanza a sense of panic is evoked: a movement in the water heralds the return of the spirits to the surface and the speakers take to flight, terrified that they may be caught.

The poem consists of six stanzas in an effective tripping metre of amphibrachs which convey a sensation of suspense and quick movement. Each stanza has 6 lines rhymed a b a b c c, the fifth (of only two syllables) being an exclamation or question.

l. 9. **dem Zauberer, gilt es zu Leid:** they are mourning the . . . magician.

l. 16. **schwirren:** the whirring sound made by the wings of an insect—here used to suggest the murmuring of prayers.

l. 26. **Sie spielen in grünendem Feuer:** their fire flashes green as they dance.

l. 28. **Zum Meere verzieht sich der Weiher:** the pool stretches (i.e. seems to extend) to the sea.

l. 31. **Mitten = Mitte.** Cf. 'Der Feuerreiter', l. 42. **samt der Mützen.**

l. 33. **Es orgelt im Rohr und es klirret im Schilf:** there is a whistling and a clashing in the reeds. For the use of the impersonal verb to evoke dread cf. 'Die traurige Krönung', ll. 19, 24–7.

21. ER IST'S

Composed on March 9, 1829, during a walk at Pflummern (Karl Fischer (1) p. 85), this poem appears in *Maler Nolten* with 'Frühling, ja du bist's!' repeated as a refrain. See Baumann, II, p. 213 and (comment by Mörike) p. 214: 'Die Strophen bezeichneten ganz jene zärtlich aufgeregte Stimmung, womit die neue Jahreszeit den Menschen, und den Genesenden weit inniger als den Gesunden, heimzusuchen pflegt'. During a period of convalescence after illness, Nolten hears the words (presented as the first verse of a song) sung by the watchman's daughter. Mörike's intimate contact with Nature enables him to personify Spring and sense its approach through the organs of sight ('blaues Band'), smell, touch ('Düfte streifen') and hearing ('Harfenton').

22. DAS VERLASSENE MÄGDLEIN

Written May, 1829, this poem was introduced into *Maler Nolten* (Baumann, II, pp. 171–2): Nolten hears a woman's voice, which resembles that of Agnes to whom he has been unfaithful, singing the words, and he is moved to tears, 'ganz der Süßigkeit eines — dennoch so bittern! Schmerzens genießend'. There are interpretations by Wilhelm Schneider and Staiger. Staiger (1) identifies the girl's feelings with those of her creator: as a late-comer Mörike looks to the past, living in memory. Day is for him the present with its political and social problems ('der freche Tag' in 'Gesang zu zweien in der Nacht'), night the time of memories and dreams, love being associated with early morning as the point of return to sober reality (cf. 'Ein Stündlein wohl vor Tag'). The girl has dreamt of her faithless, absent lover and longs to return to her dream as she gazes at the sparks of the fire (an example of the elements from which Mörike feels exiled). The poem then, Staiger argues, expresses the private wish of Mörike and a whole generation faced with barren reality after a night of romantic dreams. As in other poems (e.g. 'Der Knabe und das Immlein', 'Begegnung', 'Der Gärtner', 'Agnes', 'Erinna an Sappho') Mörike separates his emotion from himself and gives the impression that he is speaking only in the name of others.

Some readers may feel that the ingenious interpretation of Staiger, outlined above, goes too far and that the poem's roots are to be found rather in the poet's experience of love (and his use of a favourite theme—infidelity). In the third stanza the girl *suddenly* remembers that she has dreamt of her lover (there is no suggestion that she will dream of him again) and in her misery she longs for the day (here life itself) to pass. Mörike seems to prefer night to day in his poetry, it is true, here day is connected in the girl's mind with monotony and duty. The beauty of the flames (stanza 2) recalls her happiest memory (her love) and hence her dream (stanza 3) which causes her to weep for an existence now without purpose (stanza 4).

Staiger (ibid.) rightly maintains that the poem is not a *Volkslied*, and continues, 'Der Ton aber ist erstaunlich getroffen. Man glaubt an Improvisation'. Much of the poem's effect derives from skilful variations in metre and rhythm. A. Heusler considers the metre and the relation to the *Ländler* (*Deutsche Versgeschichte*, Berlin / Leipzig, 1929, III, pp. 382–3). Many popular variants of the poem in Germany and Austria have been recorded (see Maync (1) I, p. 417), but these seem to originate from Mörike's version.

l. 1. **wann = wenn** (Swabian).

23. BEGEGNUNG

Written 1829, this poem reflects a sly roguishness in its author towards the intimate relationship of lovers; here the storm of the previous night is identified with the passionate embrace of the lovers. As F. Th. Vischer (p. 36) has pointed out, the poem is not popular in tone—'die Sprache ist die der Gebildeten, anmutige Betrachtung, der Stoff aber in seiner Einfachheit und unschuldigen Sinnlichkeit naiv'. See the interpretation by von Wiese (1), pp. 259–61.

l. 3. **ungebetne:** uninvited.

l. 5. **kommt...die Straßen** (archaic): comes along the street.

l. 8. **unstet:** unsettled.

l. 15. **offnen Stübchen:** the window in the room was open.

24. SEHNSUCHT

Mörike sent the text of this poem to Luise Rau on January 4, 1830, probably shortly after its composition (Rath, (3) pp. 70 ff.). The first published version (*Maler Nolten*, Baumann, II, pp. 75–6) has a number of textual differences and some verses not included in our text (that sent to Luise). The following two stanzas appeared after the second in the *Maler Nolten* version:

Wie von der Höhe nieder / Der reinste Himmel flimmt,
Der nun um Rosenglieder / Entzückter Engel schwimmt!

Und Wunderkräfte spielen / Mir fröhlich durch die Brust,
In taumelnden Gefühlen / Kaum bin ich mir bewußt.

Then followed the present third stanza, and then this stanza (after which the poem proceeded as in our text):

Wo denk' ich hinzuschweifen? / Faßt mich ein Zauberschwarm?
Will ich die Welt ergreifen / Mit diesem jungen Arm?

In the novel Nolten sets out on an exhilarating January morning to visit a royal country-seat: the landscape is covered with snow and Nolten's mood a strange mixture of joy in living and melancholy. Riding on his horse, he sings aloud the words of the poem (presented as a long forgotten song of his friend Larkens) which seem to explain to him his present feelings.

It is not possible to establish which version is the older, but the shorter text (given here) is undoubtedly the better one. The shorter version may be a revision in which weak stanzas have been omitted and imagery given greater concreteness. The title originally used in the early editions of Mörike's poems was 'Zurechtweisung', probably with reference to the gentle reproof which he gives to his heart in stanza 6. As in 'Trost', the poet communes with his heart.

The theme is a romantic one, but treated in an unromantic manner. As in other early poems (e.g. 'An einem Wintermorgen . . .') the early morning brings visions to the poet: he is in tune with Nature (inspired by dawn at first, later attributing to it his own sense of inspiration, cf. stanza 2, 'glüht', 'Berauschte Nebel'). In the third stanza the effect on his whole being ('Geist und Sinn') is expressed in the precise imagery of golden arrows winged through space which represent his longing. Romantic ways of satisfying his desire for activity are imagined in the next two stanzas, the chance occurrence of the word Love in his thoughts bringing him back to earth to meditate upon the original source of his intoxication, the happiness which love conveys to him. In the last stanza his longing finds its goal—the presence of the beloved. The metre appears conventional, 3 beat iambic rhymed a b a b, but the sense permits variation of stress, e.g. l. 17, Stúrzt' ich mich bráusend nách! and l. 22, Hérz, hast du nícht bedácht.

l. 5. **Felsen = Fels.**

l. 23. **mit eins:** all at once.

ll. 27–8. She (Love) draws back gently into her toils the confused notes (of his song).

25. KARWOCHE

Written in 1830, the poem also appears in a slightly different form (together with sonnets to Luise which it resembles in metre and rhyming system, cf. 'Zu viel') in *Maler Nolten* (Baumann, II, p. 380) where the fifth stanza runs:

> Wird sie sich dann in Andachtslust versenken
> Und sehnsuchtsvoll in süße Liebes-Massen
> Den Himmel und die Welt zusammenfassen,
> So soll sie mein — auch mein! dabei gedenken.

Mörike perceives a striking contrast between the solemn lament of Passion Week and the joyous mood of nature at springtime: he bids the birds be silent, for his beloved picks violets to adorn the altar, not herself, and seeks her bridegroom in Christ, not the poet. For this reason Love and Spring have disappeared for the poet and lost their meaning. Religious practice is divorced from the seasonal rebirth and the flowering of human love.

26. ZU VIEL

Written 1830, this poem is one of a number of sonnets addressed to Luise Rau, others being 'Liebesglück', 'Am Walde', 'Nur zu!', 'An Luise' and 'An die Geliebte'. An earlier version is introduced among a collection of poems in Larkens' papers in *Maler Nolten* (Baumann, ii, pp. 377 ff.) and here the second stanza runs:

> Wenn ich den Blick nun zu den Bergen richte,
> Die duftig meiner Liebe Tal umhegen —
> O Herz, was hilft dein Wiegen und dein Wägen,
> Daß all der Wonne herber Streit sich schlichte!

The poet is tormented by the magic both of Nature and of Love; he pleads with each force to help him resolve his problem with the other and characteristically longs to seek refuge in night. The first stanza is remarkable for the sensuality of its imagery; for the sonnet form cf. 'Antike Poesie', but here all rhymes are feminine and the rhyming scheme in the last 6 lines is different.

27. ELFENLIED

Written 1831, and introduced into *Maler Nolten* in 'Der letzte König von Orplid', scene 13 (Baumann, ii, p. 134). The poem, composed in an intimate and mockingly humorous vein which has a special appeal for children (of all ages), tells the story of a sleepy elf who mistakes the watchman's cry 'Eleven o'clock' for a call to him: drunk with slumber he totters away, takes the lights of glow-worms for lamp-lit windows and bumps his head on the wall trying to look in (elves being traditionally inquisitive). For an interpretation see Stahlmann. The lines are varied in length and rhymed a b a b c c d ('orphan') e e f f g g h h i i j j i i k k.

l. 4. **wohl um:** at (common in *Volkslied*).

l. 7. **Silpelit:** a mischievous elf in Mörike's mythology.

l. 9. **begibt sich vor sein Schneckenhaus:** comes out of the snail-shell in which he lives.

l. 11. **Sein Schläflein** (humorous diminutive) **war nicht voll getan:** he had not slept his fill.

l. 12. **humpelt . . . tippe tapp** (onomatopoeia): staggers sleepily.

l. 14. **Schlupft = schlüpft** (Swabian): slips, hops.

l. 15. **der Glühwurm** for plural (collective).

l. 16. **Was sind das helle Fensterlein? = Was sind das für . . .**

l. 18. **Die Kleinen:** the elves.

l. 19. **treiben's:** have a good time.

l. 21. **Pfui** — expression of disgust. **stößt = er stößt.**

l. 22. **gelt = nicht wahr?** (Swabian).

l. 23. **Guckuck:** the call of the cuckoo, used by children when hiding like 'Peepo!'; here, however, it is an expression of mockery by the storyteller at the elf's discomfiture.

28. AGNES

Written 1831, this poem has many features reminiscent of *Volkslied*; these include colloquialisms, the repetition of phrases to suggest an echo, irregularities in the trochaic metre (these are subtly devised, e.g. l. 11 **Mir kranken Blut** and l. 23 **Von seiner Hand**) and variation in the length of the line (4 beats, 2 beats, 3 beats, the scheme being repeated within each stanza). The theme of infidelity is a prominent one in Mörike's poetry. The poem appears in *Maler Nolten* (Baumann, ii, pp. 275–6) as a song sung by Agnes which reflects, as the context reveals, her fears that Nolten may desert her.

The girl's lost happiness is symbolized in the passing of the rose season and her present misery is contrasted with the merry mood of the harvesters. She moves as in a dream, and is drawn back to the spot where her lover plighted his troth: her rose ribbon, a keepsake from him, flutters in the wind (itself associated with inconstancy for Mörike, cf. 'Lied vom Winde').

ll. 4, 5. blieben = geblieben.

l. 6. Sollte mir nicht bangen: I should not be anxious (afraid), cf. 'es ist mir bang'.

ll. 7, 8. wohlgemut: cheerfully.

ll. 10, 11. kranken Blut = krankem Blut: sick girl, cf. 'das junge Blut', young person.

l. 13. Schleiche = ich schleiche.

29. VERBORGENHEIT

Written in 1832. The poet desires seclusion from too much love of the world, not from hatred of it; solitude will protect him from excess of joy in the moment and of pain at its passing. The mixture of ecstasy and melancholy in his experience of life is expressed in the haunting lines of stanzas 2 and 3. The final stanza is a repetition of his prayer to the world. Although the verse form (4 line trochaic stanzas rhymed a b b a) is not uncommon, it is deliberately chosen as best conveying the pensive sadness of mood and the renunciatory gesture of the poem. For a sensitive interpretation see Staiger (4) pp. 23-4.

l. 7. immerdar: always (archaic).

l. 11. Schwere: melancholy, heaviness (cf. M.H.G.). so = die (relative, now archaic—cf. M.H.G.).

l. 12. wonniglich in meiner Brust: this line refers to 'Freude zücket'. wonniglich: ecstatically; for form cf. bescheidentlich 'Auf der Reise' l. 20.

30. SEUFZER

Written 1832. Towards the end of *Maler Nolten* (Baumann, II, p. 389) Agnes and Henni sing 'die kraftvollen Strophen eines lateinischen Buß-liedes aus E-dur'. The Latin poem is presented as the beginning of this hymn and the translation appended in a footnote with l. 7 'War Eis im Herzen' instead of the later version in our text. Mörike found the original in an old song-book, *Geistreiches Gesangbuch, den Kern alter und neuer Lieder wie auch die Noten der unbekannten Melodien . . . in sich haltend*, ed. Joh. Anast. Freyling-hausen, Halle, 173– (Renz, p. 104). He took only the first stanza, consider-ing it to be far the best. Writing to Karl Mörike on February 22, 1832, he quotes a translation which is at least his fourth attempt:

> Dein Liebesfeuer, / Jesu, wie teuer
> Wollt ich es hegen, / Wollt ich es pflegen!
> Habs nicht geheget / Und nicht gepfleget
> In meinem Herzen — / O Reueschmerzen!

He then remarks: 'Die sieben ersten Zeilen sind leidlich, aber die letzte ist matt gegen das Mark und Bein durchschneidende O frigus triste'. After considering other possible translations ('O bittre Schmerzen', 'Falschheit im Herzen, o Höllenschmerzen', 'war falsch im Herzen') he continues: 'Kalt' geht nicht wegen des entgegengesetzten sinnlichen Begriffs von Hölle, außer ich würde durch die stärkste Antithese einen größeren Sprung von einem Bilde zum andern machen' (Seebaß (1) pp. 318-20). On February 26th he asked Vischer for a translation, expressing dissatisfaction with his own: this was Vischer's version, sent on March 27th (Robert Vischer, p. 64):

Mein Heiland treu und gut, / Von deiner Liebesglut
Entbrennen sollt ich, / Dich lieben wollt ich —
Warum entbrannt ich nicht? / Liebend umwand ich nicht?
Retter in aller Not, / Herz ist so kalt und tot!

The theme is related to that of 'Wo find' ich Trost?', the song which follows it in *Maler Nolten*. For other translations by Mörike see 'An den Schlaf', 'Akme und Septimius' and the collections of translations from Theocritus and Anacreon.

31. GEBET

Date of composition uncertain; probably written about 1832, first published in 1848 edition of poems. Its note of resignation to God's will recalls that of 'Verborgenheit' and 'Zum Neuen Jahr'. Mörike, who knows the dangers and torments of an excess either of joy or of sorrow, pleads for the happy mean in what is allotted to him ('holdes Bescheiden'). The second stanza appears as the morning prayer of Agnes in *Maler Nolten* (Baumann, II, p. 375). Since the rhythm and rhyming scheme change in the second stanza, it is possible that the second stanza was written first or that two poems have been fused into one.

l. 1. **willt** = **willst** (archaic). Bithell (2), p. 14, has pointed out that here Mörike 'literally repeats a line of Luther's Bible ("Herr, wie du wilt, so schicks mit mir")'.

l. 3. **vergnügt:** content.

l. 8. **Mitten:** cf. 'Die Geister am Mummelsee', l. 31.

32. ZUM NEUEN JAHR

Written in 1832 for the New Year 1833 with a note that it should be sung to a melody 'Wie dort auf den Auen' (from Anton Salieri's opera *Axur*); see Mayne (1) I, p. 430, and Koschlig (2). The treatment of a religious theme in this occasional poem is semi-erotic, yet the piety and acceptance of God's will, prominent in poems of this period and later, are sincere. There are touches of baroque imagery (the cupid-like angel and the blue pavilions of the heavens with moons and suns) and the delicate rhythm of the metre (amphibrachs, as in 'Der Gärtner', but with a feminine ending to every line) is admirably suited to the theme; rhyme a a b c d e e e c.

33. ABSCHIED

Written in 1837, this humorous poem originally concluded Mörike's collected poems from the second edition onwards. Mörike sent a copy to Hermann Kurz on June 6, 1837 (Kindermann, pp. 36–7); this bore the original title 'Der kommt nimmer'. Both Mörike and his correspondent disliked reviewers at this time, and here the poet is sharing a private joke with his friend. The reviewer has not been invited to examine the author's work ('Unangeklopft', l. 1) and looks only at the author's shadow, not his real self, draws attention to his nose and chatters in the hope of extracting confessions: the author is pleased to see him depart and, after helping him down the stairs with a little kick from behind, pretends to be surprised at the suddenness of his visitor's descent! Lines of varying length are used, generally with three lines rhyming together at the end of each stanza (stanza 1 has 11 lines, stanza 2 13). Cf. Goethe's poem 'Der Rezensent'.

l. 7. **Auswuchs:** protuberance (the reviewer must find something to criticize l). **is = ist.**

l. 8. **alle Wetter—;** l. 9, **Ei Hasen!;** l. 20, **Alle Hagel!**—exclamations of surprise.

l. 11. **so eine Weltsnase:** a nose of such importance.

ll. 20–1. **Gerumpel . . . Gepurzel . . . Gehumpel:** thumping, somersaulting, limping.

34. AN MEINEN VETTER

Written June 1837; the cousin is an invented type through whom the poet pokes fun at his fellow-Swabians, and a little at himself. Mörike addresses him in the old-fashioned third person singular form 'Er'. The first section (13 lines) is a general observation; the second (19 lines), the story of a chance meeting, has a more personal note. The meal at the inn is described with the enthusiasm of a gourmand; these details, like the references to the small talk, tooth-picking, smoking and keeping an eye on the horses, all suggest the enjoyments and occupations of ordinary life. In the final section (5 lines) Mörike recalls the tragic transitoriness of human life, even for one so firmly rooted as his cousin. A 4 beat unrhymed trochaic metre is used.

l. 3. **Sommerwesten:** 'summer-waistcoats', an invented word and perhaps a joking allusion to the 'sunny' trait of their nature.

ll. 7–8. **Rechnungsräte, Revisoren Oder Kameralverwalter:** various officials, say 'accountants, auditors or officials in the department of finance'.

l. 11. **Petit-maîtres = Stutzer:** dandies.

l. 16. **Post:** the inn at Besigheim, a small town near Heilbronn, once Post Station between Cleversulzbach and Ludwigsburg.

l. 21. **Radieschen:** (little red) radishes.

l. 23. **von der neusten Zeitung:** about the latest news.

l. 28. **auszustochern:** to pick (teeth).

l. 31. **dampft und diskuriert:** puffs at his pipe and discusses. **inmittelst:** now and then.

35. AN MEINEN VETTER

(AN DENSELBEN)

Written May 1840, this poem usually follows the other of the same title, which it resembles in several ways, including the old-fashioned form of address and the metre; it is, however, composed in a lighter vein and jokingly points a moral against too narrow an interest in one field (cf. 'Häusliche Szene').

l. 12. **sich . . . balbieren trachtet:** intends to shave.

l. 29. **Überdem:** what is more. **förmlich:** actually, really.

l. 34. **sich Kröpfe lachen:** *lit.* to laugh till they get goitres, say 'laugh their heads off'.

36. DER KNABE UND DAS IMMLEIN

Written 1837; Karl Fischer (1) p. 131, points out the connection with a little house in a vineyard ('Vogeltrost' see 'Der alte Turmhahn', l. 186) near Cleversulzbach. Mörike liked to visit the place and may have composed the poem there. Woodtli-Löffler remarks on the enigmatic character of the first stanza, with its reference to a house without doors or windows, and the extension of the metre with 'windebang' in the second line (a feature of every stanza); her suggestion that the first stanza may be the beginning of another poem, introduced here to stress the desultory narration so typical of the *Volkslied*, is a possible explanation. Trümpler (p. 37) has shown that Woodtli-Löffler was wrong in supposing that 'windebang' has anything to do with wind: it is dialect tautology, as in Swabian 'wind und weh', 'very anxiously'. The mood of anxiety, waiting and boredom in the first stanza prepares the reader for the sultry silence of the second, in which the bee appears. The youth, watching the bee, recalls that the girl he loves has a beehive in her garden and asks the bee whether it has been sent by her as a messenger to him. The bee replies in the negative, revealing now for the first time to the reader that the girl is still young ('kaum aus der Schule' l. 18), knows nothing of love and has scarcely seen the youth, who has presumably admired her from a distance. The girl's youth and innocence are further underlined in stanza 6, where the bee declares that her mouth is already watering at the thought of the honey he will bring. The youth replies that love-making is the sweetest and most pleasant thing on earth, far sweeter than honey. The poem has echoes of folk-song, especially in stanza 3. In stanza 2 the effect of spontaneity is achieved through the initial 'Und'. Rhyme a b c b, cf. 'Der Gärtner'.

l. 4. **Die Weile wird ihm lang:** it is bored.

l. 9. **Mein Lieb:** my darling, to which 'ihm' (l. 21) may refer.

37. DER GÄRTNER

Written 1837. The difference in rank between the lover and the woman he adores is a conventional situation in *Volkslied* and romantic poetry (cf. 'Schön-Rohtraut' and Eichendorff's 'Der Gärtner' in *Aus dem Leben eines Taugenichts*). In the first stanza the gardener admires the lady from afar, in the second he dare not look at her as she passes, but gazes at the sand he has sprinkled on her path; after she has ridden past, he watches her hat bobbing up and down (stanza 3), while in the climax of the final stanza his mood is one of complete surrender—he prays inwardly for a single feather or blossom from her, offering thousands of blossoms in return. The verse form is in the *Volkslied* style, 4 line stanzas rhymed a b c b in amphibrachs, and is well suited both to convey the simple thoughts of the lover and to suggest the movement of the horse.

l. 1. **Leibrößlein:** own (personal) horse, cf. 'Leibarzt'.

38. DIE SOLDATENBRAUT

Written 1837. The naive tone of the *Volkslied* is well suited to the speaker and her situation, the simple enumeration of the soldier's 'decorations' in the last stanza being a joking commentary on his apparent deficiencies in the second.

l. 3. **ließ' er sein Blut:** he would give (sacrifice) his blood.

l. 8. **Abschied:** discharge.

l. 11. the lovers are bound by a pink ribbon given as a keepsake.

l. 12. **Hauskreuz:** a nagging housewife (here used jokingly). F. Th. Vischer uses the word in this sense in a letter to Strauß of 1848 (*Briefwechsel zwischen Strauß und Vischer*, ed. Adolf Rapp, Stuttgart, 1952, I, p. 208).

39. DER TAMBOUR⁄

Written in 1837 and also in *Volkslied* style, this poem, like 'Die Soldaten-braut', begins with a wish. The drummer boy indulges in dreams of delight; if his mother were a witch, she should accompany his regiment to France as the canteen-woman ('Marketenderin', l. 4) and then all his simple accoutrements could be turned into food and drink or be used for them. The idea that this magic transformation would have to take place at midnight makes him think of the moon (whose light he will need) and hence of his beloved. Since she is far away, however, the misery of his loneliness and hard life in a foreign land suddenly returns, shattering his *Wunschtraum*. The poem consists of 10 rhymed couplets (with some dialect rhymes, e.g. **könnt'**/ **Regiment, fehlt/Gezelt, End'**/**könnt'**, cf. 'Lied vom Winde' ll. 21–2) in a metre of 4 beats to the line. Although the metre is mainly iambic, an anapaest is sometimes to be found.

l. 5. **wohl um:** cf. 'Elfenlied' l. 4.

l. 13. **Humpen:** tankard, bumper.

l. 14. **Burgunderblut:** Burgundy (wine).

l. 17. **auf Französ'ch:** in French, a humorous reference to the fact that he is in France.

40. AN EINE ÄOLSHARFE

The motto is taken from Horace, *Odes* ii, No. ix, ll. 9–12, addressed to C. Valgius Rufus (a poet, known to Horace, of the circle of Maecenas) on the death of Mystes (probably a favourite Greek slave): 'You ever in tearful strains dwell upon your Mystes taken from you; and the sorrows of your love fail not when the morning star is rising nor when he flies before the coursing sun' (translation by Lonsdale and Lee, *The Works of Horace*, London, 1890). Horace's poem is concerned with friendship between two men and the grief of one at the death of the other. Hermann Kurz admired the motto and wrote of the poem: ' "Die Äolsharfe" besonders ist ein poetischer Triumph, wie ihn noch wenige errungen haben, und hat eine musikalische Malerei, daß man die ganze Szene Ton für Ton in sich schlürfen kann' (Kindermann, p. 167, 28/9/1838).

Mörike wrote the poem in 1837, probably in the spring on the occasion of a visit to Ludwigsburg. He addresses the Aeolian harp whose music he associates with a personal loss similar to that of Rufus, the death of his younger brother August in 1824 at the age of seventeen. August had died as an apothecary's apprentice at Ludwigsburg; after a visit to this town Mörike wrote to Luise Rau: 'In der Emichsburg hörte ich die Windharfen flüstern, wie sonst: die süßen Töne schmolzen alles Vergangene in mir auf' (Rath (3), p. 174, 14/5/1831). His sorrow at August's death was deep and enduring, and he referred to it several times in letters, even in later years. Most critics now agree that the setting for the poem, in so far as it is identifiable, is in Ludwigsburg; the ivy-covered wall of the terrace, by which an Aeolian harp was sometimes placed, was the Emichsburg in the grounds of the *Schloß*, while the 'frisch grünendem Hügel' (l. 11) is August's grave in the cemetery in the distance; between the grave and the palace grounds are gardens with fruit trees whose blossoms are carried over by the wind in spring to fill the air with fragrance and rustle in the strings of the harp. See also Hirsch (1) and (2). Aeolian harps were owned by Justinus Kerner and the poet's cousin Karl Mörike of Neuenstadt: the instrument is also mentioned in *Maler Nolten*. In a letter to Gretchen Speeth and his sister Klara (Seebaß (2) pp. 219–20, 3/5/1848) the poet remarked that he had often heard the music of the Aeolian harp at the Emichsburg when he was a boy.

The poem is thus inspired by a visit to a place familiar to him in his youth which reminds him once more of August: it is written in free verse embodying elements from various classical verse forms with lines of varying length—see Kaiser (p. 111). As his translations in *Klassische Blumenlese* (composed in the last half of the eighteen thirties, published 1840) demonstrate, Mörike was particularly interested in classical metres at this time. For perceptive interpretations of the poem see v. Wiese, pp. 219–20 and Beck (1). See also a valuable note by Thiele.

There are three sections in the poem, these being of 7, 11 and 7 lines respectively. In the first the poet implores the harp to begin again (l. 6) its lament (which he remembers from childhood). As the harp gives forth music, he addresses the winds which cause the melodies and which come from the direction of August's grave; they strew the fragrance of spring blossoms and make music, so that his heart is oppressed by a longing attuned to the rise and fall of the melody. Here the wind is perhaps to be thought of as a messenger or link bringing something of August's being (if only in memory) to Mörike. This would accord with the image of destruction in the third section, when a gust of wind scatters the petals of the beautiful rose at the poet's feet, the same gust causing the harp to emit a cry which finds its echo in Mörike's soul, thrilling him with its sweetness and yet, by its act of destruction, reminding him of how transitory beauty is and how vulnerable before death are both youth and beauty.

41. AN MEINE MUTTER

Written 1837: cf. Heine's sonnets 'An meine Mutter' (*Buch der Lieder*). Elegiac couplets are used.

l. 1. **gilt dir:** is meant for you.
l. 4. **vernehmbar:** audible.
l. 5. **unmutig:** angrily.
l. 6. thinks of the abiding peace of his heavenly part.

42. AUF EIN ALTES BILD

Written 1837; for theme cf. 'Schlafendes Jesuskind'. In development the poem passes from the general (peaceful summer scene in green landscape—the setting) to the special (Virgin and Child) and these are linked through the final reference to the growing tree from which the Cross will be made. The thought here is a moving one, and its effect is heightened by the simplicity of form (rhymed couplets) and by language which is devoid of pose or affectation.

l. 3. **Schau:** look (S. German). **das Knäblein Sündelos:** the Christ-Child.
l. 5. **wonnesam:** blissfully.

43. TROST

Written in 1837; the poet's reaction to a mood of despair. In the first stanza (exposition) a humorous tone is employed to mask real distress; in the second Mörike addresses his heart (a mediaeval touch), introducing various similes to indicate the intimate relationship between himself and this essential part of him. In the third and final section (ll. 21–3) he finds new courage in a determination to remain firmly united with his heart, a suggestion made in the second stanza. For the metre (4 beat, trochaic, unrhymed lines) cf. 'An meinen Vetter' (1837, 1840).

44. EIN STÜNDLEIN WOHL VOR TAG

Written in 1837, this poem has characteristics of the *Volkslied* and the mediaeval *Tagelied* in theme and form (see Maync (1) 1, pp. 412–3). In poetry a bird is frequently encountered as the messenger for lovers. Here the swallow addresses the girl in the second stanza, but she does not wish to hear of her lover's infidelity, although her final remark suggests that she believes the bird's message. The burden 'Ein Stündlein wohl vor Tag' recalls 'Drei Stündlein vor dem Tagen' of 'Es wollt' ein Jäger jagen' in *Des Knaben Wunderhorn*. The rhyme of the burden is taken up in each stanza, a device which gives unity to the whole poem.

l. 1. **Derweil = während** (archaic).

45. JÄGERLIED

Written in December, 1837. Hunting is a conventional occupation for the lover in the tradition of the *Volkslied*, see 'Schön-Rohtraut' and 'Der Jäger'. D. F. Strauß expressed his admiration for the poem in the famous comment, 'Mörike nimmt nur eine Hand voll Erde, drückt sie ein wenig und alsbald fliegt ein Vögelchen davon' (Strauß (3), p. 55—letter to F. Th. Vischer of March 15, 1838). At the wish of a composer Mörike later appended a third, inferior verse which was not included in the collected poems: see Karl Fischer (1), p. 132.

46. THEOKRIT

Written in 1837. Mörike became closely acquainted with the work of Theocritus in 1828. Theocritus soon became one of his favourite poets, and in 1855 he collaborated with Friedrich Notter in a translation of his idylls; see Baumann, 1, pp. 427–73. The poem is composed in elegiac couplets.

l. 3. **die Chariten:** see Idyll XVI, Baumann, 1, p. 468, ll. 6 ff.

l. 7. cf. 'Die Zauberin', Baumann, 1, pp. 432 ff. (also for **Hekates Künste,** l. 8).

ll. 9 ff. **junge Herakles:** a reference to another poem in the collection translated by Notter. **Herakles-=**Hercules.

l. 11. **Kalliope:** the Muse associated with epic poetry.

47. MÄRCHEN VOM SICHERN MANN

Although the poem was written in 1838, its origins go back to Mörike's student days, the theme being first mentioned in his letters in 1824. The fragment preserved of a letter written in the summer of 1825 contains the germ of the poem. It is mentioned that, towards the end of his life, 'der sichere Mann' had the *idée fixe* of becoming a prophet and arrived in Hades with a collection of 'Stubentüren' under his arm, tied together to form a kind of book, from which he was resolved to read his lectures: there is also a refer-

ence to an attempt by Satan to make the listeners laugh by his pranks and to
'der sichere Mann' pulling out his tail and using it as a bookmark (see Karl
Fischer, (1) p. 125). 'Der sichere Mann' is also mentioned in 'Der letzte
König von Orplid' sc. 5 (*Maler Nolten*, II, pp. 114–15) and was a private
joke in Mörike's circle (cf. Kindermann, pp. 88 ff., 92). Sending the poem
to Hartlaub on February 13, 1838, the poet wrote (Renz, p. 69): 'Zugleich
folgt ein heroisches Gedicht vom sichern Mann: es ist ungefähr die Geschichte,
die ich Euch schon in Tübingen preisgab und wozu ich damals eine Zeich-
nung machte, deren Du Dich auch noch erinnern wirst. Zeig das Gedicht
weiter niemand und sage nichts davon, ich will in der Sammlung unseren
Kreis damit überraschen'. Strauß disapproved of various features in the
poem, including the pulling out of the devil's tail (cf. letters to Vischer
(Strauß (3) pp. 52 f.) and to Mörike (Maync (3) p. 104). In reply to Strauß
Mörike wrote on February 12, 1838 (Walter, pp. 594–5): '[Um] noch einmal
auf die Philosophie vom sichern Mann zu kommen. Es kann wohl sein,
daß ich die Sache früher etwas anders erzählte, indessen weißt Du ja, . . .
wie sich ein Mythus im Lauf der Zeit bald besser, bald schlechter formierte.

Ich glaube übrigens, Du wirst Dich mit dem Schlusse noch versöhnen.
Ich nahm den Teufel, neben dem ungleich größern Suckelborst doch immer
auch als einen Kerl von übermenschlicher Größe an; deshalb jener am
Schwanz wohl ein klein wenig ziehen darf. Eine Art von Prophezeiung
im Munde des Sichern Mannes habe ich jederzeit mit diesem Anlaß verknüpft;
auch scheint sie nötig, um die mit dem Ganzen etwa zu verbindende Idee
einigermaßen hervortreten zu lassen'. The poem was illustrated by Moritz
von Schwind (see Rath (1)).

As F. Th. Vischer (p. 40) has pointed out, the clumsy giant is a favourite
character in German literature. Although Mörike probably drew inspiration
from the Cyclops and his cave in Homer's *Odyssey*, from Theocritus' idyll
'The Cyclops' (which he translated, see Baumann, I, pp. 455–7) and from
Shakespeare's figures (e.g. in *Midsummer Night's Dream* and *Tempest*), the
legend as a whole displays considerable originality by the poet. For useful
comment see Maync (1), I, pp. 421–2, v. Wiese (1), pp. 137–43, Trümpler,
pp. 90–6, Guardini, Wilhelm Schneider and Heinsius, pp. 217–9. Heinsius
considers the poem to be a joke directed against Schelling's *Naturphilosophie*,
with Suckelborst an obvious reference to the character in Schelling's poem
Epikurisch Glaubensbekenntnis Heinz Widerporstens' and the pulling out
of the devil's tail three times his 'dreifache Potenzierung'. When the gods
laugh at the prophecies of 'der sichere Mann', Heinsius suggests, Mörike
is making fun of his own beliefs as they are reflected in 'Die Elemente'.
With the help of Lolegrin, the divine entertainer of the gods who brings
light with him (cf. l. 27), Suckelborst awakes from inorganic to organic
life, illustrating Schelling's maxim, 'Die Schwere wirkt auf den Keim der
Dinge hin, das Lichtwesen aber strebt, die Knospe zu entfalten'. The solemn
tone of the hexameters contrasts amusingly with the humorous treatment of
the theme.

l. 2. **etliche = einige.**

l. 5. **Sündflut:** the Flood.

l. 8. **Unhold:** ugly person.

l. 12. **es starret der Bart ihm:** his beard is stiff.

l. 13. **Igelslocher Balbierer:** the barber of Igelsloch, a village near
Hirsau.

l. 14. **woselbst = wo.**

l. 17. **bei nächtlicher Weile:** at night time.

l. 21. **Blachfeld:** open country (field).

l. 23. **Konterfei:** image, likeness.

l. 25. **saftstrotzende:** succulent.

l. 26. **vertragsweis:** according to an arrangement (treaty).

l. 31. **Weyla:** native goddess of Orplid.

l. 32. **Küchenschelle:** pasque flower, Anemone Pulsatilla.

l. 34. **Suckelborst:** *lit.* pig bristle.

l. 37. **ein Halbgott:** Serachadan his father was divine, with immortal strength, cf. l. 43 below.

l. 56. **hohen Gesichten:** sublime visions.

l. 71. **Schattengefild':** Hades.

l. 77. **Begeisteter:** person endowed with intelligence. **Schweinpelz:** smutty (nasty) fellow—term of abuse popular in Swabia.

l. 80. A reminiscence of student pranks with the rafts on the Neckar in Tübingen.

l. 81. **zum Torten:** causing injury to.

l. 83. **Keulers:** wild boar.

l. 86. **jegliches = jedes, alles** (archaic).

l. 88. **Schmeidige:** make supple.

l. 91. **geoffenbart:** has been revealed (to Suckelborst before his birth, cf. ll. 56 ff.).

l. 93. **Leg . . . es aus:** expound (interpret) it.

l. 101. **die Galle verraucht:** his anger had died down.

l. 122. **Schöne = Schönheit:**

l. 123. **Forchenwalde:** pine forest (**Forche = Föhre**).

l. 127. **Kunkelstuben:** the rooms where the women forgather to spin.

l. 131. **zween = zwei.**

l. 133. **denn = als** (Swabian).

l. 135. **den Kloben:** the piece of wood barring the door.

l. 141. **die Tenne gelüftet:** the threshing-floors aired (because the barn doors had been removed).

l. 144. **Öhre:** eyelets or sockets in which the door hinges are inserted.

l. 148. **des schwer Entwandelnden Fußtritt:** the heavy footsteps of the giant moving away.

l. 156: **Flecken:** village (Swabian).

l. 157. **mir:** cf. use in 'Häusliche Szene', ll. 2, 8.

l. 160. **kein Schweif:** no tail (humorous for animal).

l. 171. **Schlafratz:** sleepy-head (a rather stronger term of abuse in German than the English equivalent).

l. 173. **bleuen:** beat (M.H.G.).

l. 184. **sinnigen:** thoughtful.

l. 186. Translate: 'artistically overlaid with red laths crosswise'.

l. 190. **unnachsagbaren Sprachen:** inimitable languages.

l. 195. **Tief aufschnaufend:** with a deep breath (of relief).

l. 204. **gewundenes:** winding, sinuous—a graphic image.

ll. 207-8. **unliebsames Kehrricht / Niederen Volks:** unpleasant sweepings of the lower orders.

l. 218. **für sich:** on their own.

l. 221. **Weltbuch:** book of world knowledge (philosophy).

l. 222. **Schrecken:** here neuter form used.

l. 224. **Hummel:** here 'bull'.

l. 228. **genüber** = **gegenüber.**
ll. 234 ff. repetition of ll. 58 ff.
l. 240. **Dämon:** spirit.
l. 242. **gehörnete** = **gehörnte.**
l. 260. **Schanden** = **Schande.**
l. 262. The devil has his own hell, separate from Hades.
l. 281. **basta:** enough, that will do (used in Swabian).
l. 288. **in Gestalt der Zikade:** in the form of the cricket.

48. SCHÖN-ROHTRAUT

Mörike wrote to Hartlaub (Renz, pp. 74–5) that he composed this poem in bed on the morning of March 31, 1838; his remarks to Schwind thirty years later, when he is discussing moments of inspiration evoked by some triviality, suggest that he may have had the verses already in his head before that time (Rath, (1) p. 126) and are of particular interest. 'Das stärkste dieser Art (moment of inspiration) ist die Entstehung der Ballade Rohtraut. Ich stieß einmal, es war in Cleversulzbach, zufällig in einem Wörterbuch auf den mir bis dahin unbekannten altdeutschen Frauennamen. Er leuchtete mich an als wie in einer Rosenglut, und mit ihm war auch schon die Königs-tochter da. Von dieser Vorstellung erwärmt, trat ich aus dem Zimmer zu ebener Erde in den Garten hinaus, ging einmal den breiten Weg bis zur hintersten Laube hinunter und hatte das Gedicht erfunden, fast gleichzeitig damit das Versmaß und die ersten Zeilen, worauf die Ausführung auch wie von selbst erfolgte'. Kurz (Kindermann, p. 151) wished Mörike to alter Ringang (possibly derived from the name 'Oll Rinkrank' in *Grimms Kinder- und Hausmärchen*) because it conveys 'einen kurios humoristischen Eindruck'; this is, however, the case with most of Mörike's invented names, which appeal to his sense of irony.

Writing to a friend in 1873 shortly before his own death, Strauß ((3), pp. 569 f.) made the following illuminating remarks concerning the poem and his attitude to it. 'Von Meistern lernen wir immer und in allerlei Weise. Zunächst natürlich an ihren Mängeln. Besonders lehrreich aber ist, wenn wir, was uns erst als Mangel erschienen war, als Vorzug erkennen können. So hatte ich gegen das oben angezeigte Gedicht infolge meiner Schwärmerei für natürlichen Ausdruck längere Zeit ein Vorurteil. Seine altertümliche Sprache wollte mir gemacht erscheinen. Wollte ich die Richtigkeit dieses Urteils prüfen, mußte ich in die Grundidee des Gedichts einzudringen suchen. Denn ging jene Sprache aus dieser Grundidee hervor, so war sie natürlich und nicht gemacht. Schön-Rohtraut ist ein Mädchen, das in einem Fall nicht die Strenge und Spröde macht, weil sie weiß, daß sie an sich streng und spröde ist; ein Herz, das es wagt, einmal mit sich selbst zu spielen, weil es weiß, daß es sich in der Hauptsache fest und sicher in der Gewalt hat. Und in dem Knaben hat sie sich nicht getäuscht, hat eine der ihrigen verwandte Natur gefunden. Das Gedicht ist von einer strengen Keuschheit, einer herben Süßigkeit, einer gesunden, gefaßten Kraft, die eine eigene Form verlangte. Ohne Anklang an die Sitten in moderner Zeit muß es auch seine Sprache aus der Vorzeit nehmen. Selbst im Versbau hat der Dichter eine gewisse Härte und Starrheit mit zartestem Wohllaut zu mischen gewußt'.

Mayne, (2), pp. 353 ff., rightly considers that each stanza can be divided into 5 lines of *Aufgesang* (introduction) and 3 lines of *Abgesang* (burden) with the retarding fifth line as the dividing point; both sections have a refrain which appears in each stanza, the *Aufgesang* l.2 (variation in stanza 3) and the *Abgesang* l. 8 'Schweig stille, mein Herze!' which is also a skilfully employed *leit-motiv*. 'Das "Schweig stille" im Munde des Knaben bedeutet in der ersten Strophe hoffnungslose Entsagung des Abseitsstehenden, in der zweiten Beschwichtigung einer mächtigen Sehnsucht auf Grund erfolgter Annäherung, in der dritten das jähe Stocken des Herzschlags ob des unvermuteten Kusses und in der letzten das Gelöbnis unverbrüchlicher Geheimhaltung der genossenen Seligkeit, die, so kurz sie äußerlich bemessen war, doch das ganze Leben des Liebenden und Geliebten durchglühen und überglänzen wird.'

This poem spans Mörike's poems in the manner of the *Volkslied* and his ballads; the situation is similar to that in 'Der Gärtner', one typical of the *Volkslied* and *Minnesang*—the man loves a woman hopelessly, for she is far above him in rank. The youth's love grows until he can scarcely control the emotion; the princess sees his love and grants him a kiss in stanza 3—a stanza with a distinctive note in the variation of the refrain (l. 2). The climax comes in the final stanza with the youth's sense of triumph and of an achievement far beyond his dreams.

The influence of *Volkslied* is particularly obvious in the language and the system of rhyming which only applies to half the lines, each stanza rhyming a b c c d e e f, the lines being varied in length.

Storm's attention was first drawn to Mörike's poetry through 'Schön Rohrtraut' which his friend Theodor Mommsen 'discovered' in a periodical. The poem was translated into English by George Meredith (1850).

l. 9. **über eine kleine Weil'**: after a little while.
l. 17. **Einsmals = einmal, einst** (archaic).
l. 19. **wunniglich = wonniglich**: pleasurably, blissfully.
l. 22. **vergunnt = vergönnt**: granted, allowed.

49. IM WEINBERG

A first version, entitled 'An Klara' (dedicated to Mörike's sister), is similar to this revised text of 1838; as compared with the first version the introduction has been shortened, l. 10 has been inserted, the last line changed (formerly 'Ahnungsvoll, wie im Traum, die holde Seele, versunken') and some less important textual alterations made. Written in hexameters, the poem reflects the workings of Mörike's poetic fancy: the butterfly's contact with the copy of the New Testament leads to the idea of the insect receiving blessing (presented with gentle humour, l. 15) and endowing the lily in the beloved's garden with 'Geist und himmlisches Leben'. For the conception of mystic power emanating from a flower and the introduction of the butterfly cf. 'Auf eine Christblume'.

50. DER ALTE TURMHAHN

Written from 1840 onwards, this poem in the first version consisted of only 22 lines, with a drawing of the weather-cock and the title 'Aus Gelegenheit der Kirchthurm-Renovation im Juli 1840' (this occurred at Cleversulzbach, referred to as 'Klepperfeld' at this stage in the poem). In a letter to Storm of April 21, 1854 (Seebaß (1), p. 729), Mörike mentioned that he acquired the weathercock (still to be seen in the Schiller Nationalmuseum, Marbach) when he was vicar, but that he altered the character of the priest, making him more venerable and giving him a wife and family; the poet continued, 'Das Ganze entstand unter Sehnsucht nach dem ländlich pfarrkirchlichen Leben'. In 1845 Mörike added a few verses, including the description of the stove, but only completed the poem in 1852, impelled by nostalgic memories of his life as a country parson (he had retired from the Church in 1843). See Maync (1) 1, pp. 434–5, and v. Wiese (1), pp. 241–4. Written in *Knittelvers* (cf. 'Erzengel Michaels Feder') the poem displays Mörike's humorous gift at its best. Like the weather-cock, Mörike himself was torn between a desire for security (he sensed the dangers of life) and an occasional wish for wider experience, and he here pokes fun at this conflict in himself in which (a *Biedermeier* trait) discretion usually prevails.

l. 7. **falber**: livid, blue-grey.

l. 8. **bereift**: covered with hoar frost.

l. 13. **für Alter**: with age.

l. 14. **Glitz und Glanz**: glitter and shine (note alliteration).

l. 16. **abgesetzt**: deposed.

l. 17. **Meinthalb**: an expression of grudging acceptance.

l. 19. **Stolzier', prachtier'**: prance, show off.

l. 20. i.e. the wind will pay court to you in a way different from what you expect.

l. 25. **spat** = spät.

l. 27. **hinterdrein**: behind them.

l. 28. **Bastes Evlein mit dem Schecken**: little Eve Baste with the piebald horse (the surname is sometimes put first in this way in country districts where the family is more important than the individual).

l. 31. **Drecklein**: bird-dropping. **itzt** = jetzt.

l. 32. **beschmitzt** = beschmutzt.

l. 33. **Hochwürden**: plural form of address normally used in addressing ecclesiastical dignitaries.

l. 39. **krummer Teufelshöcker**: crooked devil of a hunchback.

l. 40. **schätz'**: think (Swabian).

l. 43. **preßhafter** = bresthafter: infirm, decrepit.

l. 44. **fuhr ab**: slid down from.

l. 45. **schnurrt' hinein**: whizzed in (to the belfry).

l. 46. **glotzten**: gaped. The bells, hanging in safety, are not moved by the weather-cock's plight.

ll. 49–50. **tät . . . überweisen**: handed over.

l. 51. **zween Batzen**: two pennies. **meint Wunder**: thinks (Swabian).

l. 52. **Plunder**: junk.

l. 58. **Unachtend**: not heeding.

ll. 64 ff. Translate: I should deserve ill fortune, were I not to . . .

l. 69. **Lümmel**: rascal. **schnell bedacht**: quickly mindful of his own interest.

l. 71. **Es fehlt' nicht viel, so tat ich . . .**: I almost . . .

l. 78. **Göckel** = Gockelhahn (Swabian 'Gögele'): cock, chanticleer.

l. 81. **Gottesmann**: parson. **mildiglich**: gently, kindly.

l. 84. **nachpolteret**: tramps noisily after.

l. 87. **sondre** = besondere: special, choice.

ll. 88–9. Humorous effect achieved by compounds. **Reseda**: mignonette. **Schmack**: smell (Swabian), scent.

l. 90. **Rüchlein**: whiff.

ll. 100 ff. The description of the stove recalls the technique employed by Homer for a shield in the *Iliad* (Book XVIII, ll. 486 to end) and for the hero's cap in the German mediaeval story in verse *Meier Helmbrecht* (ll. 14–103).

ll. 108–19. The legend of Archbishop Hatto of Mainz, who, it is said, caused a number of poor people (whom he compared to mice bent on devouring his corn) to be burned in a barn during a famine; he was then attacked by mice (and rats) and sought refuge in the *Mäuseturm* at Bingen on the Rhine, but was eaten alive by them.

ll. 120–3. The story of Belshazzar's feast; see 'Book of Daniel', ch. 5.

ll. 124–39. Abraham and Sara; see 'Genesis', ch. 18.

l. 103. **ausstaffiert:** dressed up.

l. 105. **Dieweil:** as, since.   **Hort:** place of refuge, shelter.

l. 106. **Kind und Kegel:** everybody.

l. 108. **Platten:** weak dat. sing. fem. Cf. **Mützen,** 'Der Feuerreiter', l. 42.

l. 111. **Ziefer** = **Ungeziefer:** vermin.

l. 112. **richten** = **ausrichten:** perform, do.

l. 115. **an der Mauer auf:** up the wall.   **sie:** the rats and mice.

l. 120. Imagine the inserted 'Hier seht ihr' of l. 108 (this applies also to l. 124). **Sodann:** next. **König Belsazars seinen Schmaus:** this construction, a pseudo-archaism, is a contamination of a genitive construction with a dative one (e.g. 'dem König . . . seinen Schmaus').

l. 121. **Saus und Braus:** riotous revelry.

l. 124. **Zuletzt da vorne:** last (of the pictures) in the front. **stellt sich für:** introduces herself, is introduced.

l. 129. **sich Lachens nicht entbrach:** couldn't help laughing.

l. 130. **hoch betaget:** advanced in years.

l. 133. **geschicht** = **geschieht.**

l. 134. **hinwieder:** in reply. **Flausen machet:** tells fibs.

l. 138. **leugt:** denies (cf. M.H.G. 'lougen').

l. 146. **fangt an** = **fängt an.**

l. 147. **anderst mag's nicht sein:** that's how it has to be.

l. 150. Translate: his text already stirs him.

l. 151. Translate: on which he tacks his work together (**zu Faden schlagen,** a milliner's term).

l. 152. Translate: now and again, in the meantime.

l. 154. **Sternenlüfteschwall:** flood of air from the starlit night—an invented compound.

l. 155. **Mit Haufen:** in clouds, great quantities.

ll. 156–7. **Verrenberg . . . Schäferbühel:** mountains near Cleversulzbach.

l. 160. **sein Alpha und sein O:** a pious tribute to the Almighty by the parson. Cf. in the carol 'In dulci jubilo': 'Qui est A. et O', '(he) who is Alpha and Omega'.

l. 161. **Exordio:** introduction in sermon (**Exordium**).

l. 162. **Postament:** post (Swabian).

l. 166. **sacht eine Prise greifet:** softly takes a pinch of snuff.

l. 167. **roten Butzen:** burnt-off end (of wick).

l. 168. **zieht er vor sich:** he recites.

l. 169. **vernehmentlich:** audibly.

l. 170. **So:** relative, cf. 'Verborgenheit', l. 11.

l. 171. **bringe . . . zu Kropf:** take note of (*lit.* 'bring to my maw').

l. 173. **Applicatio:** application of the Word to life.

l. 176. **Ruckt** = **rückt:** pushes back.

l. 178. **Im Finstern:** in the darkness (**das Finstere**).

l. 180. **Registratur:** desk.

l. 181. **Totenuhr:** death-watch beetle.

l. 184. **stieben:** fly like dust.

l. 186. **im Vogeltrost:** cf. note on 'Der Knabe und das Immlein'.

l. 187. **sich erbost:** rages.

l. 188. **jähling:** suddenly.   **mit Knallen:** cracking.

ll. 190 ff. Here Mörike pokes fun at the smug bourgeois outlook to which, as he knows, he is himself prone.   **lobt man sich . . . dankbarlich:** one is thankful for.

l. 192. **wärmelt halt:** gives warmth (all through the night).

l. 198. **herentgegen = dagegen.**

l. 212. **die Lis':** Liza, the maid.

l. 219. **Klause:** cell, study.

ll. 220–1. Translate: not to pay visits, drive around in his coach, make his *Schnaps* or potter about in other ways.

l. 223. Translate: Once—don't let it go any further.

l. 225. **Meisenschlag:** cage for a tomtit.

l. 229. **zur Kirchen:** weak fem. sing. dat. Cf. **Platten,** l. 108.

l. 231. **Sakristei:** vestry.

l. 238. **beschaut sich:** has a look at.

ll. 239–40. **Kinderlehr':** catechism. **Oblatenschachtel:** box for consecrated wafers. **Amtssigill:** seal of office.

l. 242. **Zuteuerst = sogar. Grus = Gries:** fine sand. **besicht = sieht.**

l. 244. **frank = frei.**

ll. 248 ff. Johann Valentin Andreä (1586-1654), Swabian theologian and poet: Johann Albrecht Bengel (1687-1752) known for his edition of and commentary on the New Testament. There were several theologians named Rieger, including Georg Konrad Rieger (1687-1743), his son Karl Heinrich Rieger (1726-91) and Immanuel von Rieger (1727-98). Christoph Friedrich Oetinger (1702-82), Swabian theologian whose works were popular with Mörike. Philipp Friedrich Hiller (1699-1769), composer of hymns and writer of work on harp playing (**Harfenspiel**).

l. 253. **so fehlt nicht viel:** it almost does.

l. 261. **eingenickt:** dozed off.

l. 269. **Flecken:** cf. note to 'Märchen vom sichern Mann', l. 156

l. 274. **verwichen:** recently.

ll. 276–7. **Bogen:** bow-front. **brüstet sich:** brags. **hoffärtig:** arrogantly.

l. 281. The double negative is Swabian.

l. 283. **geil:** arrogant, vain.

l. 287. Translate: puts . . . and you as well on the runners (of the sleigh).

l. 289. **der ganze Käs':** the whole lot.

l. 290. **Scherb:** old, useless creature (literally a broken piece of pottery).

ll. 292–3. Translate: Think about yourself, think of your end! You won't exist for another hundred years.

51. WALDPLAGE

Written 1841; the humorous effect is heightened by the use of a classical metre, the iambic trimeter or senarius, which is in glaring contrast to the unpoetic theme (the poet is attacked by 'Schnaken', a vigorous species of gnat, while reading Klopstock's odes).

l. 3. **Er = der Wald.**

l. 4. **reißend:** rapacious, ravenous.

ll. 17 ff. The gnat has six legs (here popular form 'Füße')—that is why,

Mörike jokingly remarks, he has chosen the classical senarius, a metre of six feet.

l. 21. **Rüssel:** proboscis.

l. 25. **ungestalten:** misshapen.

ll. 32 ff. References to Klopstock's odes 'An Fanny', 'An Cidli,' 'Der Zürchersee', 'Die frühen Gräber' and 'Der Rheinwein'.

ll. 34 ff. Mörike declares that an even bigger and more troublesome kind of gnat exists on the Rhine.

l. 43. **Zwillings-Nymphen-Paar:** twin trunks forming a rest for the poet's back (mentioned l. 30).

l. 51. A line from 'Die frühen Gräber', altered slightly to fit the metre.

l. 53. **Canaille:** a term of abuse, 'rascal'.

l. 64. **etwelcher:** some. Cf. Gottfried Keller's poem 'Die kleine Passion' (1872).

52. AUF EINER WANDERUNG

For the first version, entitled 'Auf zwei Sängerinnen' and dated August 12, 1841, see Leffson, IV, pp. 250–1: this is an occasional poem of uneven quality, 42 lines in length, in which the poet introduces two travellers and allows them to express their admiration for the beautiful voice of Marie Mörike, wife of his cousin Karl Mörike. Our version, written 1845, consists of a first stanza which is mainly a 'purple passage' in the earlier poem and a second stanza which is almost entirely fresh composition. The whole testifies to the intoxicating effect on Mörike the poet of the beauty he experienced in nature and music.

After the sober opening lines, revelation comes with the melodious sounds of the bells and of the single voice: these transfigure the poet's natural surroundings. In the second stanza, Mörike loses himself in visions of colour and melody, thanking the Muse for having breathed into him a love for the world which brought him this experience. See Brigitte Müller (pp. 10–11) and Adorno. The two stanzas differ in length, rhyming system and metre, the latter having a complicated and varying rhythm.

l. 10. **lustbeklommen:** the mixture of pleasure and anxiety in ecstasy often experienced by the poet.

l. 14. **Gewühle:** welter of colour from the setting sun.

l. 15. **in goldnem Rauch:** cf. Hölderlin's 'Patmos' ll. 28 ff. (Maync).

l. 16. **Erlenbach:** *lit.* a brook flanked by alders.

53. AUF EINE CHRISTBLUME

Writing to Hartlaub from Cleversulzbach on October 29, 1841 (Renz, pp. 153–5), Mörike described how, on a visit to Neuenstadt on the day before, he had found in the churchyard, on a grave familiar to him, a flower for which he had sought in vain for years: it was in bloom and had five somewhat broad petals, which were folded right back and resembled those of a lily in their whiteness and robustness; these were light green at the tips and a deeper green in the calyx. The stamens at the centre formed a pale yellow ball, adorned at the top with four or five short purple threads. The stem was round, muddy-green and spotted with red, bent so that the flower was close to the ground. The leaves were also a muddy green, the scent 'äußerst fein, kaum bemerklich, aber angenehm'. Mörike continued: 'So reizend fremd sah sie mich an, sehnsuchterregend!'

When his sister Klara, who accompanied him, identified the flower as a
Christmas rose, he was delighted. The flower was taken away by them.
Having arrived home, Mörike consulted his 'Gartenbüchlein von Pastor
Müller', learnt that the flower is among those which blossom early ('schön, daß
es früh[en] heißt, nicht spät[en], so duftet sie schon wie von dem anderen Jahr
herüber, was einer so mystischen Blume wohl zuzutrauen ist') appears in
November, December and January, can endure the coldest weather ('dies
ist der besonders schöne Zug an ihr!') thrives in sandy soil and likes shade
or a wintry spot, dying, however, in a warm or sunny place. Mörike placed
it in a glass by the window, 'und zwar in den schönsten Mondenschein, in
dem es ihr besonders wohl und leicht zu atmen schien'. He then continued:
'Sie freute mich unbeschreiblich, und schon dachte ich daran, meine Emp-
findungen bei guter Zeit in einigen Strophen auszudrücken — kann wohl
auch noch geschehen — doch unrecht Gut soll nicht gedeihen [his sense of
guilt at having taken the flower from the grave]. Heute vormittag, nachdem
ich sie den Morgen noch begrüßt, warf sie der Wind unvermerkterweise
aus dem Glas auf die Straße und war nicht mehr zu finden. (Wenn sie jetzt
wieder auf dem Grabe stünde! In der Tat gedenke ich ihrer jetzt nur wie
eines lieblichen Geistes.)'

Felix Braun (*Das musische Land*, Innsbruck, 1952, p. 144) relates that
Stifter, visited by the young Rosegger, preferred to talk of the beauties of
Austrian landscape after he had drawn the curtains to shut out the view,
so that he might speak from memory. Similarly Mörike only wrote his poem
after the flower had disappeared. The objective yet imaginative approach is
in striking contrast to that of Lenau in his 'Primula veris' where the poet
reads his own fate into that of the flower. It is hoped to show in the notes
below that many *motifs* in the poem are already foreshadowed in the letter
above. Mörike's consciousness of a mystical aura surrounding the flower
and his use of religious imagery (the Catholic tendency arises from aesthetic
considerations) develop naturally from his own experience and what he had
read of the flower. For interpretations see v. Wiese (1), pp. 72–9, Mare, pp.
137–41, and Storz. The mystic power of the flower and the introduction of
the butterfly are anticipated in 'Im Weinberg'.

I. Storz has shown that the stanzas of the first part of the poem fall into
definite sections by reason of their content: this view can be confirmed from
a close examination of the metre.

The first two stanzas are a delighted greeting of the flower and a reflection
as to how it came to be on the spot where Mörike discovered it: it prefers
shade ('Tochter des Walds'), resembles the lily in some respects, and has
long been sought by the poet. His reverence for the flower is increased by
the fact that it is unknown to him and that he finds it at a barren, wintry time
in a churchyard other than that of his own home. In this reference to
'fremden Kirchhof' Mörike allows himself poetic licence, but even more so
in the next stanza where he pretends not to know the identity of the person
buried in the grave and imagines how the flower will bring blessing to the
unknown.

The third stanza stands alone: here a mystical romantic setting for the
flower in keeping with its characteristics is portrayed. The fourth and fifth
stanzas (a third section) return to the flower itself. It flourishes under moon-
light, but not in the sun (see letter), it is nourished by cold air: its fragrance
from the yellow centre ('goldner Fülle') is scarcely perceptible, it recalls
the bridal dress of the Virgin Mary, an association with the Christmas scene

derived from its name and the season in which it blooms. In the sixth and seventh stanzas the association with Christ is extended, and, in contrast, the realm of nature is introduced in the figure of the elf, typical of one aspect of the poet's own mythology. The five purple drops are not necessarily based on the memory of another flower, as Storz maintains; they may be suggested by the filaments (mentioned in the letter) with which Mörike decorates the flower in imagination (hence 'würden') as a reminder of the Passion. The elf, on his way to a fairy dance at midnight in a glade, feels reverence at the aura ('Glorie') of the flower and does not dare to approach it, despite his curiosity (a characteristic of elves, see 'Elfenlied').

At first sight the metre appears to be a regular iambic one of 5 beats to a line; closer examination reveals that in ll. 1, 7, 8, 13, 14, 15, 21 a more natural reading is gained by stressing the first syllable and beginning with a dactyl. In some cases (ll. 7, 14, 15) the previous line ends in an unstressed syllable so that the verse flows on; in others (ll. 8, 13, 21) a pause is indicated, either to underline a parallel (l. 8 with l. 7) or to show that a new section begins (ll. 1, 13, 21). Metrically stanza 3 is linked with the first two stanzas. The metre and rhyming system, seldom used by Mörike elsewhere, allow him, through the rhymed couplets which are alternately feminine and masculine, to give subtlety and music to a simple form.

II. Here Mörike turns his thoughts to the butterfly who will only come to full development in the spring: perhaps the poet is thinking of himself and his devotion to the 'Goethezeit' in this reference to the late-comer who will never taste the nectar of the flower. The poet likes to imagine that perhaps the insect's spirit, invisible to him, is encircling the flower as it blossoms. In these two stanzas Mörike keeps the metre of I, but changes the rhyming system to a b b a: ll. 32, 33 may be regarded as commencing with a stressed syllable.

54. AN WILHELM HARTLAUB

Composed in 1842 and sent to Hartlaub, this poem expresses sincerely Mörike's affection for his closest friend. Hartlaub was a talented pianist, and Mörike was deeply moved by music. In a letter to Waiblinger of 1822 he wrote: 'Wirklich tut die Musik eine unbeschreibliche Wirkung auf mich — oft ist's wie eine Krankheit, aber nur periodisch. Ich sage Dir, eine bewegliche, nicht gerade traurige Musik, oft eine fröhliche, kann mir manchmal mein Innerstes lösen. Da versink ich in die wehmütigsten Phantasien, wo ich die ganze Welt küssend voll Liebe umfassen möchte, wo mir das Kleinliche und Schlimme in seiner ganzen Nichtigkeit und wo mir *alles* in einem andern, verklärten Lichte erscheint'. Mörike's thoughts move from the music itself to the player and his own love for him. The idyllic scene in the last section is an attempt to conquer this excess of feeling, perhaps to mask it from the reader by a diversion. The length of the sections vary ((1) 6 lines: (2) 8: (3) 10: (4) 6: (5) 4). Rhymed couplets are used with an iambic line normally of 5 beats (for variety ll. 11, 18, 29 have been lengthened to 6 beats).

55. DIE SCHÖNE BUCHE

Written in 1842 and sent to Hartlaub in a shorter, slightly different form on August 29, 1842. Like other short idylls (e.g. 'Waldidylle') the poem is composed in elegiac couplets. See the interpretation of Guardini, who points out that the poem consists of two sections, one of seven, the other of eight couplets, the first a portrayal of the scene, the second Mörike's experience of the place. The poet is brought to this remote spot (l. 1, l. 16 'Ab dem Pfade gelockt', l. 17 'Hain' suggesting Nature hallowed by a divine presence) by the spirit of the grove, and the place seems to be awaiting and receiving him, so that he hesitates in reverence, finally standing by the tree and listening to a daemonic and unfathomable stillness at midday which is in no sense gloomy or menacing. Guardini also shows that Mörike masks the shattering nature of the experience by using apparently harmless words taken from the sphere of the idyll, e.g. l. 17 'freundlich', l. 21 'zierlich'.

Mörike's failure to penetrate into Nature's secrets reflected in earlier poems ('Besuch in Urach', 'Mein Fluß') may be said to have changed his approach to Nature. Now he experiences the divine in Nature, worshipping there and resigning himself to the realization that certain things must remain hidden from him. He does not importune Nature, but awaits a sign from her. Nature herself creates beauty without the need of artistry (l. 8). Security and balance are symbolized in the tree whose shadow offers protection from the blinding sun (ll. 25–6) and whose 'roundness' is continually stressed (l. 5 'Rings', l. 6 'umher', l. 8 'Rund')—see Spitzer (p. 143, note 2) to suggest this very security and balance. See also v. Wiese (1), pp. 44–7.

l. 3. **gediegenem**: solid, robust.

l. 14. **die Hellung:** here 'brightness', 'light'—an area where the light is not obscured by growing trees.

l. 17. **auflauschende:** listening attentively, on the alert.

56. FRÜH IM WAGEN

The first part of the poem was written on a journey in 1843, and in 1846 the whole was revised and extended. See Goes (3) and Schaeffer (pp. 74–9) who compares it favourably with Liliencron's 'Heimgang in der Frühe' and Carossa's early poem 'Heimweg', stressing the remarkable effect of the catalectic metre and masculine rhymes and noting unconscious echoes of the mediaeval *Tagelied*. The alliterative 'sch' in each line of stanza 3 gives the stanza unity and suggests the dreamy mood of the poet—at this point he turns from contemplation of the dawn to memories of his beloved at the moment of parting the night before. He is brought back to reality by the appearance of the sun and the breaking of the illusion is humorously underlined by a sudden shower of rain. For theme cf. 'Auf der Reise'.

57. ABREISE

Written 1846. See Jacob, pp. 34–7 and v. Wiese, pp. 266–9, who rightly maintains that the poem bears the stamp of the later Mörike. The scene is conveyed to the reader in remarkably lucid and concrete terms: the theme of parting, popular with Mörike, is here treated with greater objectivity and subtlety than in earlier poems like 'Auf der Reise': it is employed to present a graphic scene and to reveal the instability of the young woman's feelings—her outburst of grief at the departure of her lover gives way to laughter before the sun has time to dry the streets after the summer shower!

The poet begins his poem by creating a mood of impatience: the coach must start, but one passenger has not arrived. The sudden shower and its effects occupy our attention from l. 5 until the arrival of the young man, whereupon the earlier atmosphere of haste is resumed (l. 12). The sense of urgency disappears when interest is centred upon the dry patch on the road (l. 14 onwards), the lateness of the young man's arrival is explained, while the climax of the poem comes with the presentation of the girl and her fickle behaviour. Unrhymed, trochaic 5 beat lines are used.

l. 8. **Letzung:** refreshment.
l. 18. **angezeigt:** proclaimed, marked.
l. 29. **Wildfang:** wild young girl, madcap, tomboy.

58. AM RHEINFALL

On September 25, 1840, Mörike wrote to Hartlaub, 'Wir kommen heute von Schaffhausen, und ich bin noch ganz voll von der Herrlichkeit des Rheinfalls, den wir den gestrigen Tag vom Frühstück bis zum Sonnenuntergang genossen haben' (Renz, p. 121). In August 1846 he sent Hartlaub 'Rheinfall bei Schaffhausen' (our poem) with the remark: 'Donnerstag, den 30. Juli morgens 10 Uhr, schrieb ich diese Verse, wozu mir die gebrauchten Bilder, wie ich glaube, sich in unmittelbarem Anschauen der Natur aufdrangen, auf meine Schiefertafel nieder, trat halb noch in Gedanken mit dieser neu in mir belebten Erinnerung beschäftigt, an das Fenster...' (ibid., p. 261). The sense of power in the rushing water seems then to be an emotion recollected long after the experience. The poem, written in elegiac couplets, has a plasticity and objectivity of presentation which makes it a striking contrast to Lenau's poem on the Niagara Falls, 'Verschiedene Deutung'. Concerning the difference Hoffmeister (pp. xxix-xxx) writes: 'Bei Lenau muß es der Niagarafall sein, die poetische Sensation! Aber weshalb, wozu? Was gibt der Niagarafall her? Nichts als zwei dürftige Gleichnisse des menschlichen Ich, die jeder Poet an jedem beliebigen Wasserfall hätte ablesen können! Bei Mörike ist es der 'Rheinfall'. Doch in diesem Gedicht finden wir nichts von romantischer Ichbezogenheit. Da ist vielmehr mythisches Eigenleben Gestalt geworden. Da ist nichts Seelisches ausgesagt, entsubjektiviert; da wird vielmehr das Objekt in sich selber lebendig; da sagt das Objekt selbst etwas aus. Da spricht Leben zu Leben, Geist zu Geist'.

The poet tries to prepare the visitor to the falls for a shattering experience: his own heart, he declares, was almost borne away in joy (as though by the water), while he received, both visually and aurally, an impression of tumult —here a giant, fallen from the sky, would not hear his own cry of rage. Mythologizing, the poet sees the cascading water as innumerable horses of the gods storming downwards and spreading their silver manes (foam and spray) at the foot of the falls, seeming always the same and yet different. The overwhelming nature of the impression is strengthened by the use of images like 'gewaltigen Händen', 'Gigant' and 'Götter'. Mörike cannot bear to await the outcome, should there be one (he is now absorbed in his poetic fancy). Suddenly he feels dread ('Angst') and, as if to confirm his fears, the vault of the sky overhead is rent by thunder. Cf. Goethe's description of the falls in *Reise in die Schweiz*, especially the following passage: 'Leichte Windstöße kräuselten lebhafter die Säume des stürzenden Schaumes, Dunst schien mit Dunst gewaltsamer zu kämpfen, und indem die ungeheure Erscheinung immer sich selbst gleich blieb, fürchtete der Zuschauer dem Uebermaß zu unterliegen und erwartete als Mensch jeden Augenblick eine Katastrophe' (Weimar edition, XXXIV, 1902, p. 365). For an interpretation of the poem, see Steigerthal.

59. AUF EINE LAMPE

Written in 1846, this *Dinggedicht* is remarkable for the perfect harmony of its content (portrayal of a work of art) and its form (iambic trimeters). The poem has aroused much critical interest in recent years, see v. Wiese (1), pp. 221–3, Staiger (2) and (3), Spitzer, Graham, Stahlmann, Wilhelm Schneider, Nordheim, Pollack and Guardini. The controversy revolves around the interpretation of the famous last line. Staiger sees the poet as a late-comer who is afraid to venture a positive assertion like Goethe's 'Die Schöne bleibt sich selber selig' (*Faust*, II, l. 7403); hence he moves away from the object (thus 'ihm') and uses 'scheint' (seems). Heidegger thinks that 'scheint' means 'shines' (of the lamp's light) and Nordheim agrees, rightly dismissing the objection that the lamp is probably not lit ('das Scheinen gehört zum Dasein der Lampe wie selbstverständlich hinzu; den Schein des Schönen aber trägt sie als Kunstwerk auch dann noch in sich und verbreitet ihn um sich, wenn ihr Lichtglanz längst erloschen ist'). Spitzer shows that 'scheint' might be interpreted in the Swabian sense as 'schön, prächtig sein' and Swabian dialect would also explain the difficult 'ihm' (for 'sich') which, as Nordheim observes, may have been chosen deliberately to avoid too great an accumulation of s-sounds in the line. Graham sees the influence of Schiller's aesthetics in the poem. A comparison with Keats' 'Ode on a Grecian Urn' throws into prominence the contemplative and idyllic tone of the verses.

Still unremoved ('noch unverrückt') the lamp hangs from the ceiling of an almost forgotten room (perhaps a ball-room, 'Lustgemach' connotes the baroque and *précieux*); it consists of a marble bowl in which is worked in bas-relief a picture of a crowd of children dancing merrily in a ring, while an ivy wreath encircles its edge. The children provide joy with their laughter, the form of the lamp a serious note. 'Reizend' (l. 7) means here 'evoking our emotional response'. 'Ein Kunstgebild der echten Art' (l. 9) might be interpreted, in view of Mörike's devotion to beauty (which he finds remote from life, cf. 'Die schöne Buche') as an embodiment of the beautiful. The last line could be taken as meaning that the beautiful is content to give forth beauty and does not need admiration or even attention. A pencil sketch by the poet dedicated to Gretchen Speeth pictures a lamp in the classical style. At the time the poem was written Mörike was turning in particular to Greek and Latin literature for inspiration, as other poems of the same year testify (cf. 'Götterwink', 'Datura Suavolens', 'Weihgeschenk' and 'Inschrift auf eine Uhr'). Critics have pointed out the double alliterative connection in the last line (schön . . . scheint; selig . . . selbst).

60. NEUE LIEBE

Written 1846, first published in the 1867 edition of poems, 'Neue Liebe' appears in the second edition of *Maler Nolten* (Baumann, II, p. 546). In the first stanza the poet asks himself whether a perfect relationship with another human being is possible; after long reflection he concludes that it is an unrealizable ideal. Unsatisfied he repeats the question and suddenly experiences the joy of inspiration and intuition; might he not have immediately the kind of relationship he desires—with God? (stanza 3). The idea engenders in him a romantic mixture of pleasure and terror, and at that moment the solution seems so clear to him that he is amazed it should have been a mystery.

'Auf der Erde' is a *leit-motiv*, the poet's problem is related to earthly existence. The rhyme and metre exemplify Mörike's artistry; the rhymes of the first stanza are repeated in the other stanzas, with inversion of rhyme half way through the poem, so that the last line rhymes with the first, i.e. 2 b b   a b b   b b a   b b a. The metrical system runs:

l. 1. 5 beat iambic.
l. 2. 3 beat dactylic-trochaic.
l. 3. 7 beat iambic.
l. 4. 5 beat iambic.
l. 5. 3 beat iambic.
l. 6. 7 beat iambic.
l. 7. 4 beat dactylic-trochaic.
l. 8. 4 beat dactylic-trochaic.
l. 9. 5 beat iambic.
l. 10. 5 beat iambic.
l. 11. 6 beat iambic.
l. 12. 5 beat iambic.
ll. 1–2. **des andern . . . sein:** belong to one another.
l. 12. **zu eigen:** as one's own.

61. HÄUSLICHE SZENE

In this poem, written 1852, the contrast between the metre (elegiac couplets) and the trivial theme (the schoolmaster and his wife have a dispute about his hobby—the making of vinegar!) is most effective, particularly as a knowledge of classical metres would be expected in a schoolmaster. Despite the quarrel the reader is never allowed to lose sight of the bond of affection which links the characters. Note the intelligent handling of dialogue and 'stage directions'. See Maync (1) 1, pp. 441–2. The *Präzeptor*, a teacher lower in rank than the *Pädagogarch* (l. 28) or *Studienrat* (l. 36), makes several kinds of vinegar, numbering the various bottles; his wife takes vinegar for pickling from the wrong bottle (one containing an experimental brew).

l. 1. **Kukumern:** cucumbers (Swabian—also used by Kerner).
l. 2. **eingemacht:** pickled. **mir:** cf. l. 8 and 'Märchen vom sichern Mann' l. 157.
l. 3. **Maß:** about a quart.
l. 12. **hält es . . . vor:** shows it.
l. 16. **mit Not:** with difficulty.
l. 17. **dich einrichtetest:** settled.
l. 19. **Stockbrett:** shelf for pot plants. **Kolben:** retorts.
l. 20. **Sommerlevkoi'n:** (annual) stock.
l. 26. **Dekanin:** wife of the dean (priest).
l. 30. **bespickt:** crammed.
l. 33. **Einwerfkäfige:** cages in which the young birds are hatched out.
l. 35. **Er dauert mich:** I am sorry for him.
ll. 37–8. **ein geschätzter Gradus:** a respected diploma (degree). Perhaps he has passed another examination.
l. 43. **geschundenen:** slaving.
l. 45. **Allotrien:** trivialities.
l. 47. **dienen:** pay back.
l. 57. **Katheder:** master's desk.
l. 60. **zeitigen:** ripen, mature.

l. 66. **Dreibätzner:** say 'threepenny bit'.

l. 67. **Der Wust der Exerzitienhefte:** the chaotic heap of exercise books (for marking).

l. 71. **vermöglichen:** well-to-do.

l. 72. **Seidenkultur:** silk-culture, breeding of silk worms.

l. 75. **die bringst du wohl gar nicht in Anschlag?:** I suppose you don't take them into account at all?

l. 77. Translate: I am an active member of three associations (for vinegar making).

l. 81. **mein Fabrikat durch sämtliche Sorten:** my vinegar in all its varieties.

l. 83. After a spiteful remark by his wife, the teacher notices that she is speaking in verse.

l. 87. Translate: Laboriously I taught you it to season harmless conversations.

l. 89. **wie dir der Schnabel gewachsen**—i.e. in your natural manner.

ll. 93–4. They cannot end their argument because of the demands of the verse form.

l. 97. The wife tricks him by leaving the distich half finished when she has had the last word, but eventually takes pity on him and completes it herself.

l. 98. **passiert:** is all right, will do.

l. 99. **Wenn er dir künftig noch besser gerät:** if you are more successful in the future.

62. ZITRONENFALTER IM APRIL

Written in 1852, or a little earlier; the imaginary speaker, the brimstone butterfly, laments its unhappy fate in being born too soon to enjoy the full fruits of life: for the poet this is a symbol of living in an age out of sympathy with true poetry and in an environment in which his poetic powers cannot attain full development. Maurer (p. 16) has quoted these lines as an example of an 'inflammable' poem of daemonic content, 'dominated as it is by the fear of death and the oppression of existence'. The use of elevated, somewhat unnatural imagery, far from veiling the serious intention, strengthens the total effect.

63. DENK' ES, O SEELE!

Written by 1852, when it appeared in *Frauenzeitung* with the title 'Grabgedanken', the poem also concluded *Mozart auf der Reise nach Prag* (1855) where it is presented (presumably fictitiously) as a Bohemian folk-song. It was given the present title when included among the collected poems. Maync (1), p. 427, mentions some general parallels to be found in the works of others. See the interpretations by Eigenbrodt, v. Wiese (pp. 132–3), Kempski, Feise, Taraba and especially Prawer ((1), pp. 12–14).

In a dialogue with himself (here with his soul, in 'Trost' with his heart) the poet struggles to come to terms with human fate as it will affect him personally, through pondering and concentrated effort he seeks to realize the inevitability of his own death and to accept the fact. The symbols introduced are those associated with life and joy. Many critics consider that by this means the poet emphasizes through contrast the horror of death: it could be argued, however, that, in introducing these symbols of living beauty (the fir-tree, the rose-bush and lively young horses) Mörike is trying to objectivize his emotions and to console himself with the thought that the beauty of life will continue after he has ceased to exist on this earth; nevertheless the principal message is 'memento mori'. The metre is unrhymed and iambic (except in ll. 6 and 14 where the stress might fall on the first syllable), each pair of lines having a unity of content and metre, 3 beat and 2 beat lines alternating. Subtle use is made of alliteration and 'word music'.

l. 1. **wo:** somewhere.

l. 13. **schrittweis:** in step.

l. 18. **blitzen:** Taraba associates the flash of light on the horseshoes with life (the iron surviving the poet), Prawer with death.

64. BESUCH IN DER KARTAUSE

Written 1861, this poem treats the inevitability of death with a gentle humour, indicating that Mörike has overcome the personal approach reflected in 'Denk' es, o Seele!': as Taraba has shown ((2), pp. 95–7), the poem is a link in development between 'Denk' es, o Seele!' and 'Erinna an Sappho'.

The typically human reaction to death (the concealment of the clock) and the tone in which the doctor tells his story both contribute to that unique blending of comedy and pathos to which the metre (iambic trimeters) is well suited. Mörike sent the poem to Paul Heyse on December 12, 1861, with the comment, 'Epistel in Jamben aparte für Dich *pour passer le temps*, ein halb elegischer Scherz, der Hauptsache nach nicht gefabelt'. Although Kloster Ittingen (near Frauenfeld in Thurgau) or Kloster Bebenhausen (if Mörike had already visited it by 1861) may have suggested a few points for the setting and the Catholic priest at Scheer, Michael Wagner (who was also a 'Pater Schaffner' or steward of a monastery at one time) given inspiration for the main character, there can be little doubt that a great deal is invented (see Hirsch, 3 and 4). It is significant in this connection that Mörike rejected the suggestion that the poem should be illustrated (letter to Krais, December 1863, Hirsch (4)), observing that no real picture of the scene existed.

Strauß ((3), p. 555, September 4, 1873) greatly admires the poem, considering it to be one of the finest poems in the collection, and the equal of 'Der alte Turmhahn'. He remarks, 'Ich möchte es eine humoristische Elegie nennen und eben dieser Gegenschein von Trauer und Scherz bringt eine zauberhaft hochpoetische Wirkung hervor'. Later he points out that the death of the Prior and 'Schaffner' is part of the disappearance of a whole world of monastic life.

Kartause: Carthusian monastery.

l. 3. **auf der Bärenhaut liegen:** to idle away one's time.

l. 9. **trotz meines schwäbischen Ketzertums.** Like many Swabians, Mörike was a Protestant.

l. 12. **Schwarten:** old books bound in pigskin.

l. 14. **Pränestes . . . Tiburs . . .:** places where Horace lived and wrote.

ll. 1–22. An introduction stressing the complete change from past to present.

ll. 23–7. The poet's comment and statement of the period of time which has elapsed between the past scene and the present one.

ll. 28–64 set the scene of the earlier visit—pleasure found in joys of life, food, wine, a collection of artistic treasures—this is contrasted with the homely clock and its grim message.

l. 28. **Weißbier:** pale Berlin beer.

l. 29. **Prälatur:** home of the prelate.

l. 33. **Laberdan:** salt cod.

l. 36. **Fürst Taxis:** the 'Thurn und Taxis' family, known for its great wealth, would presumably keep ι fine table.

l. 38. **weihrauchblumiger Vierunddreißiger:** *lit.* a wine of '34 with a bouquet like incense.

l. 39. **Halde:** slope, bank.

l. 41. **Bildschnitzerei'n:** wood-carvings.

l. 45. **Sankt Laurentius mit seinem Rost:** Christian martyr, said to have been roasted to death on a grill in Rome in A.D. 258.

l. 46. According to Greek legend, Andromeda was bound to a rock to be sacrificed to a sea monster. Perseus slew the monster and rescued her.

l. 53. **una ex illis ultima**—i.e. one of these hours will be your last hour.

l. 56. **gern von seinem Schulsack einen Zipfel wies:** who liked to show off his learning.

l. 64. **Laufst nicht, so gilt's nicht:** if you don't go (work), it doesn't count (i.e. you are no good).

ll. 65 ff. Meeting with doctor (a living link with the past) and the story from him of the last years of 'Pater Schaffner', the sudden and frightening stroke, the disappearance of the clock and the bequeathing of it to his host.

l. 78. **Beiher:** by the way, in passing.

ll. 82–3. **Es litt ihn nicht / Auswärts:** he could not bear to leave the district.

l. 83. **Enaksohn:** giant (biblical; son of Anak, 'Numbers', ch. 13, vv. 22–33).

l. 87. **Hausmannskost:** simple (plain) fare.

l. 89. **Kartäusergeist:** spirit distilled in the monastery (chartreuse).

l. 93. **Deckelglas:** a glass with a lid.

l. 94. **Schwul:** thick smoke, fug.

l. 100. **Pumpelchen:** plump little girl.

l. 103. **ein Schläglein:** a little stroke, a bit of a stroke (the diminutive ironical).

l. 110. **fackelt':** told fibs, prevaricated.

l. 114. **den Garaus . . . gemacht:** finished off.

l. 117. **sticheln:** taunt, tease.

l. 120. **stak er . . . am Spieß:** dangled on the spit, i.e. was tormented.

l. 125. **das leidige Stündlein:** the unpleasant hour, hour of death.

l. 137. **Zeitweisel:** timekeeper.

ll. 140-1. In this brief comment the poet seeks to bring out the comic aspect of the story, despite its pathos.

65. SCHLAFENDES JESUSKIND

Written 1862. On March 23, 1862, Mörike sent a copy of the poem to Hartlaub, observing that it was inspired by a picture which had been reproduced in the journal *Freya* with the brief description 'Der Knabe Jesus an einem angenehmen Schattenplatz im Freien auf einem kleinen, gewissermaßen zierlichen Kreuz eingeschlafen' (Karl Fischer (4) II, p. 274).

Francesco Albani (1578–1660), an Italian painter. For theme, cf. 'Auf ein altes Bild'. A trochaic, unrhymed metre with 5 beats to a line is used.

l. 3. **sinnvoll spielend:** in fancy fraught with meaning.

ll. 5–6. Thou flower, the glory of the Father still wrapped dreaming in the bud.

66. ERINNA AN SAPPHO

Written 1863. Zemp (1), p. 74 has called this poem Mörike's swan song, and observed, 'alles ist strengste Bildlichkeit: noch das Gesetzloseste zappelt im Netz der Form'. When asked to illustrate the poem, Moritz von Schwind refused because he thought it would be impossible 'das Unheimliche, das sie [Erinna] in ihrem Auge bemerkt, und ihr Stutzen darüber zugleich sichtbar zu machen' (Rath (1), p. 18). In metre and treatment the poem is clearly related to Mörike's translations of Anacreon (published 1864): Kaiser (p. 112) has pointed out that it begins with three Sapphics, but then changes to other forms often used by Anacreon, one of these being peculiar to him. Flad (p. 33) has shown that the information about Erinna's friendship and life in the note before the poem is incorrect, for she belonged to an era and place other than those of Sappho, although it is true that she wrote the poem named and died at the age of nineteen. The situation resembles that portrayed in 'Das Spiegelbild' by Annette von Droste-Hülshoff, while the idea of the eyes housing the spirit of life is similar to that presented in Keller's 'Abendlied'. For interpretations see Taraba (2), pp. 98–101, and Guardini.

The poem is presented in the form of a letter from Erinna to her friend Sappho; ll. 1–8 are a general introduction to the theme, ll. 9–14 set the scene, which is followed by the central event, Erinna's sudden premonition of death (ll. 15–27). Before this experience she had accepted the inevitability of death for all human beings without applying this knowledge to her own fate, she was accustomed to the idea, but not fully aware of it, just as the fisherman who has always lived by the sea does not hear the noise of the waves. Now a sudden and fundamental change takes place in her. She becomes adult in her understanding, soberly reflecting over her own inevitable end and accepting it, then thinking of her friends (ll. 28–33). In the final section she resolves to offer Sappho's present to the goddess in the childish belief (not shared by Mörike) that she may thus put off the evil day and delay her death. Note the alternation of the symbols of life and death which stresses their interrelation. Particularly effective is the image of the black-plumed arrow grazing her temples. As Taraba declares, Mörike has now reached an objective acceptance of death such as is adumbrated in the tragicomic 'Besuch in der Kartause' and which is very different from the intensely subjective attitude of 'Denk' es, o Seele!'.

l. 2. **ein altes Liedchen:** here in the sense of something universally known, accepted and perhaps half remembered.

ll. 9–12. Life is suggested in 'Sonniger Morgenglanz', 'der Bäume Wipfel' and 'Langschläferin' (association with a familiar reproach or joke).

ll. 13–14. Impression of restlessness, perhaps illness.

l. 21. **fremdendem:** estranging, alienating.

l. 24. **Wetterschein = Wetterleuchten.**

l. 37. The daughter of the Greek corn-goddess was Proserpina.